FOOD
ADDICTION

FOOD
ADDICTION

Healing
Day by Day

Daily
Affirmations

KAY SHEPPARD

Health Communications, Inc.
Deerfield Beach, Florida

www.hcibooks.com

Library of Congress Cataloging-in-Publication Data

Sheppard, Kay, 1938–
    Food addiction : healing day by day : daily affirmations / Kay Sheppard.
        p.   cm.
    ISBN 0-7573-0035-9 (tp)
    1. Compulsive eating. 2. Compulsive eating—Prevention. I. Title.

RC552.C65S4197 2003
616.85'26—dc21

                                                            2003051087

Publisher: Health Communications, Inc.
             3201 S.W. 15th Street
             Deerfield Beach, Florida 33442-8190

Cover illustration and design by Andrea Perrine Brower
Inside book design by Lawna Patterson Oldfield

Contents

Acknowledgments

Heartfelt thanks to all of the recovering people who inspire and support each other every day of their lives. Special gratitude to the men and women of The Body Knows Loop; you are my inspiration. Boundless appreciation to those who contributed their thoughts and suggestions: Al Coughlin, Rebecca Havenstein-Coughlin, Stephanie Zimmerman, Donna Birchard, Vicki Carlson, Steve Kissinger, Malcolm Broyhill, Roberta M., Barry Dansky, Kay G., Christine Blair, Georgette Valle, Tammy Kodis, Mary Ann Roesler, Kathleen Sutherland, Margie Russow, Bob Marks, Kate Costa, Danette Heuer, Diana Thomas, Judy Shepps-Battle, Karen Schmidt, Bill Murtz, Joni Gardner, Ellen Dominguez, Patty Brooks Kenny, Margot Escott, Paula Lee Andrese, Judy Moscovitz.

Thanks to the HCI staff: Peter Vegso, who has supported and encouraged books for food addicts since our first meeting in 1986; the always kind and helpful Teri Peluso; the editorial staff, especially Christine Belleris and Allison Janse; and all the editors who have assisted me over the years. Thanks to Kim Weiss and Jackie Kozlowski, who have been so helpful.

Introduction

My recovery from food addiction started with an innocent question from a friend. "Do you know that you talk a lot about food?" Before I could answer she continued, "Do you know there is a Twelve-Step program for this problem?" *Problem?* I figured. I may have had a problem, but who would want to start a program in November, right before the holiday season? What would the holidays be without my family's traditional holiday fare?

During the holiday season, I opened my bottom dresser drawer and pulled out the box of candy I had hidden there. It brought back old memories: I recalled how, as a small child, I would open the refrigerator door so quietly that my mother didn't realize I was stealing the chocolate chips or licking the icing from her cakes. By the age of fifteen, my weight had climbed to the point that I was motivated to go on my first of many weight loss programs. It was at this time that I started using cigarettes and alcohol, too. By the time I graduated college, my drinking was out of control. Eight years later, I began a recovery program and got sober. During sobriety, food became my substance of choice. I ate in private. I got so good at the deception that my husband was puzzled as to why I kept gaining weight when he only saw me "eat like a bird."

As I went to eat that candy, I suddenly felt disgusted and guilty about the way I ate. *Why was I hiding candy wrappers in the trash? Why was I sneak-eating in the bathroom? Why wasn't I sharing this candy with my family?* My friend was right: I did have a problem. That was the moment of truth when I realized I couldn't live as I had been any longer. After the holidays, I joined her at those Twelve-Step meetings in 1977. It's now been more than two and a half decades since I began my recovery. Eventually, I learned more about this disease called food addiction. For myself and others, the road is never easy nor does it stop after that initial moment of truth. In fact, I still strive to learn something new every day so that I can stay free from addictive substances.

As food addicts, we face a different challenge from people who just need to lose weight. We are recovering, not dieting. We have a disease: a physical intolerance for refined and processed foods coupled with a mental obsession. The physical intolerance is a fact—one bite of doughnut sets up a reaction that demands more binge food. That begins the cycle. For us, a food plan without a program is just a diet and diets do not work!

While I strived to get off the roller-coaster ride of food addiction, I became a licensed mental health counselor and a certified eating disorders specialist. I also developed a concept of the disease and recovery that has been useful to others who have the same addictive illness. These ideas can be found in my first books, *Food Addiction: The Body Knows* and *From the First Bite: A Complete Guide to Recovery from Food Addiction.* You'll also find the Abstinent Food Plan at the back of this book which gives you the basics for your new beginning.

This little book that you're holding is meant to be a companion to both of these books and a motivational tool to help you be successful in following the Abstinent Food Plan. This book will help you stay true to your recovery plan by helping you stay honest, open and willing each day. It will help you get organized and deal with the emotional issues you will face. Each week I provide a list of inventory questions that you can use to evaluate and correct your weekly habits. I included ones that were especially important to me, such as meeting attendance, step study, exercise and others.

Most of these cannot be ignored in order to be successful in recovery.

Along with each daily passage you'll find affirmations, which will be critical for attitude adjustment. When you read an affirmation that suits you, use the 40/40/40 method. Write it forty times, say it aloud forty times, and record it so you can listen to it forty times in your car or at home. Using the affirmations in this way will reframe negative thoughts with positive ones.

You'll also find reflections for each day that will be great catalysts for journaling. And, although the Twelve Traditions are used to guide recovery groups, they are included here as well to emphasize the importance of our personal regard for them and an awareness of our role in preserving the unity of the program.

During a group recently, a friend said, "There are no bright colors in sugar, flour and wheat." How true! These addictive substances are bland and boring. The dulled life created by those substances is a downhill ride to lethargy, numbness, illness and death. On the other hand, recovery is filled with bright colors. Life in recovery will take us wherever we want to go. There is help, hope and excitement in the process. Is it always blissful? Heck, no! Yet we can grow and change through painful times and glorious days when we have a program of discovery. No longer numb from addictive foods, we are open to the experiences of real anger, pain, joy, sorrow and happiness. With those feelings, there is an authentic life to be lived. We can feel connected to God and our loved ones. Life can be dazzling. This little volume is intended for those who strive to live that life. Hopefully it will inspire, instruct and encourage you on your way to abstinence—and life—with all its brilliant colors.

A New Beginning

In years gone by, New Year's Day was the day to make resolutions: time to start a new diet, join a gym or develop a new self-improvement plan. Usually the resolutions were the same as last year's.

Now that we are in recovery, each day is a new beginning. We focus on the new day and let the rest of the year take care of itself. We start fresh in the morning and take stock in the evening.

The great thing about being in a program is that we do not have to figure out a new diet today. We have a plan that worked yesterday; it will work today and again tomorrow. Rather than a list of resolutions, we call to mind that our resolve to stay abstinent will promote growth and change throughout the coming year. In recovery, *resolve* means that we remain committed to our goals. We no longer make any concessions to the disease. We reaffirm our focus on recovery without reservation or modification!

∽o∾

Affirmation: *I start my day with a well-thought-out plan and end my day with a thoughtful review.*

Reflection: *What growth and change do I want for myself this year?*

Getting Unstuck

No one can go back and make a brand-new start, but anyone can start from now and make a brand-new ending. If we stay stuck in old patterns because we hate to acknowledge that we need to change, pain will become our motivator. When the pain of our old habits outweighs the pleasure derived from our behavior, we search for a better way.

If we choose to make changes, we start by assessing where we are, where we need to go and how to get there. Each day, no matter how far down the path we have gone, we have to start from where we stand.

We need to take a hard look at the major blocks that bar our recovery. Those are the first to be changed. When we no longer use substances to numb discomfort and when life issues become too painful, we either grow or go.

What are our major barriers to a successful life? First, we pay attention to painful feelings that signal the presence of work to be done. Then we identify and correct issues that weaken our recovery. We identify the feelings, isolate the cause and make appropriate changes. Conscious vigilance leads us to do the next right thing!

∽o∾

Affirmation: *I identify, evaluate and correct the major blocks to my spiritual progress.*

Reflection: *What are the major blocks to my spiritual growth?*

We Abstain to Feel Better

Two irrational beliefs keep us in the disease. The first one disparages the first part of Step One—our admission of powerlessness. How can we possibly admit that we are powerless over food when we hold on to the belief that we can eat to feel better? We have deep-seated delusions that we *can* eat to feel better, that foods *can* bring comfort.

We come to realize that we eat to feel better but always feel worse. Medicating with addictive trigger foods always produces negative consequences in all areas of our lives: mental, emotional, spiritual, social, vocational, physical and domestic. The horrible consequences of addiction are progressive. Instead of creating a better life, the use of addictive foods spirals our lives downward into chaos. Abstinence is the way to feel truly better. "My true comfort food is my abstinent meal." (See page 380 of this book for an Abstinent Food Plan.)

Another irrational belief is that others are responsible for our unmanageable lives. Whenever we blame others for the pain in our lives, we redirect our focus from our true malady: addiction! When we point the finger of blame toward others, we become victims of that blame because we cannot change other people. We can only change ourselves. The wise person accepts others, and works to change himself.

∽o∾

Affirmation: Honesty is my tool for physical and emotional recovery.

Reflection: Do I continue to eat to feel better? Do I excuse or accuse others?

Failing to Plan Is Planning to Fail

We know that we have attained and maintained balance when we feel peaceful. We cannot be peaceful if we have obsessions, resentments or depression; when our eating plan is off; when we go without exercise; or when the day is disorderly.

How can we achieve peace of mind and productive days? How is that accomplished? Start with a plan: planning what to eat and eating what is planned. Schedule regular meals to maintain a level metabolism. Outline the day's tasks in a realistic manner, never scheduling too much or too little. Overdoing results in feeling overwhelmed, while underdoing results in a depressed mood and lethargy. Both open the door to the disease.

Include in your daily plan prayer and meditation time, leisure-time plans (yes, we even schedule "downtime"), brisk exercise and recovery activities. After prayer and meditation, start the day groomed and prepared with list in hand. In the evening, check the day's progress and complete any uncompleted tasks while you still have time to make one more phone call or take those vitamins! Close the day with thanks to your Higher Power for another day of recovery.

∽∘∾

Affirmation: *I write my plans for an orderly, productive day.*

Reflection: *Have I planned a day that includes the daily requirements for peaceful productivity? What are those requirements?*

Choose Freedom

People make choices every day, many of which are made without deliberation. We interact with others who drink alcohol, smoke and eat any number of unwholesome foods. When we were in active addiction, we appeared free to eat, drink and be merry, but that was an illusion. We didn't choose to eat; we ate addictively and compulsively.

When we began to abstain from addictive foods, we seemed to be losing our freedom of choice. Not so! We found that we could truly choose not to compulsively eat addictive foods, which gave us the opportunity to live another way, abstaining from addictive substances. We found our way to freedom. Just as our relatives and acquaintances have the right to choose their way of eating, we have the right to choose differently.

Being the disciplined one isn't always easy. The significant others in our lives may not appreciate our disciplined way of life. Eyes roll, comments are made or irritations expressed—sometimes loudly. No matter what others say or do, for us, choosing abstinence is always right. Freedom from compulsion, obsession and out-of-control eating is the reward.

∽०∾

Affirmation: *I evaluate and celebrate effective choices.*

Reflection: *What are my effective food choices?*

Do I Need It?

Just after the holidays, a good thing to ask ourselves is, "Is spending a problem for me?" If so, we should learn how to distinguish between our "wants" and our "needs." The momentary satisfaction of spending is destroyed by the pressures of indebtedness.

Today is a good time to start saving 10 percent of our income. Those savings can be used to reduce debt, to provide a cushion in hard times, to invest and to fund education and retirement. In order to improve financially you may wish to learn how to:

- Get out of debt and stay out of debt.
- Find areas for potential savings.
- Provide a cushion for unexpected expenses.
- Save for long-term goals.
- Stop impulse spending.

∽∘∾

Affirmation: I am financially responsible.

Reflection: Am I willing to develop a spending plan that funds my needs, an action plan for resolving my debts and a savings plan for future needs?

Let Us Write and Reflect
on the Past Week

Did I attend an adequate number of meetings?

Did I exercise too little or too much?

Did I take a Tenth Step inventory on a daily basis?

Was I accountable and honest about my food planning and implementation?

What steps did I practice?

Was I resentful, angry, selfish, dishonest or fearful?

Was I generous, kind, tolerant, patient or useful?

Were my actions, words or communications unloving or unkind?

Do I need to ask for or grant forgiveness for my actions or attitudes this week?

Was my level of hydration adequate?

Did I practice sound nutrition, including vitamins and high-quality foods?

Have I kept something to myself that should be discussed with my sponsor, advisor or therapist?

What areas of my life need improvement?

What service did I perform to help another or my group?

What was my major character flaw this week?

What was my most admirable trait this week?

Did I practice restraint of tongue and pen?

Did I rationalize any destructive behavior?

What are the corrective actions that need to be taken based on this week's inventory? Do I owe any amends?

Decisions, Decisions, Decisions

Decisions are too important to leave to chance. Recovery is based on a series of decisions.

The First Step involves a decision regarding powerlessness. If we sit on the fence regarding our food addiction, we will never be able to accomplish the dedicated work necessary to recover. We must come to a full decision that we are food addicted and cannot manage our own lives. Reservations will always lead us back into the disease.

Effective decision making is followed by an action plan. After making a First Step decision, the rest of the steps—our action plans —become possible.

∽○∽

Affirmation: *I do my recovery work with gratitude and enthusiasm.*

Reflection: *Have I fully conceded to my innermost self that I have lost control over addictive foods? Do I believe and accept that I am powerless over food and that my life is unmanageable?*

Today's Stress Buster:
Asking for the Right Things

We ask in prayer for "those right things of which we and others are in the greatest need." *Twelve Steps* and *Twelve Traditions,* p. 102. When stated in that way, how can we go wrong? Since we do not know what those "right things" might be, our prayers are effective when we ask for the "greatest and highest good for ourselves and others." Since God knows and meets our needs, why do we have to ask? Because we are benefited by the conscious contact created through prayer. The more we pray, the greater our connection to the God of our understanding.

The Twelve Steps are the spiritual principles that guide us in our personal recovery. The founders of AA came up with twelve principles—Traditions—that keep our groups intact. These Twelve Traditions are to the groups what the Twelve Steps are to the individual. They are suggested principles that ensure the survival and growth of the group. Hammered out on the anvil of experience, they were designed to guide our groups. Personal survival and survival of our program depend on understanding and implementing these principles. We need to develop a personal regard for the Twelve Traditions and an awareness of our role in preserving the unity of our Twelve Step program. In recovery, we become practitioners of the Twelve Steps *and* the Twelve Traditions.

TRADITION ONE

"Our common welfare should come first; personal recovery depends upon unity."

We definitely want a meeting to be there when we need it. Our recovery depends on that. Yet meetings disappear from time to time. What causes this disappearance? Resentments, apathy, inflated egos, complacency and relapse lead to the death of meetings. Our survival and the survival of our program depends on us. We strive to become instruments of unity in our groups. The First Tradition clearly states the primary principle of all twelve traditions: *unity*. The First Tradition is a summons to unify. Instead of a collection of separate egos, we become a group. On the group level we avoid gossip, arguments, aggression and put-downs in order to support our group. We learn to work together. Putting our personal agendas aside, we become unifiers. Our survival depends upon harmony.

∽∘∾

Affirmation: My group participation is peaceful and harmonious.
Reflection: Am I willing to discard discord for group survival?

The Fight to Be Right

Being right is a pretty powerful urge for us addicts. Certainly every war, disagreement and thrown punch starts with, "I am right, you are wrong, and you had better change!"

Sometimes we find ourselves bickering with a loved one just to prove our point. We can become so fixed on our side of an argument that we fail to see the other person's side at all. What price do we pay in the fight to be right? The price—loss of love—is high indeed. With loss of love, we lose our peace and serenity as well.

A friend shares, "Yesterday I was able to see how much I need to be right. For instance, I like to be right about the best route to take to the mall and even the right place to park so I can impress everyone with my skills. I was able yesterday to lay back and take the day as it came, not driving, not dictating recommendations (demands) unless I was asked, and it went off great: no traffic at the mall, parked close, able to walk right in to the restaurant and got a table. The real test will be when we *do* have to wait in traffic and park five blocks away. Will I be serene then?"

⋯

Affirmation: I practice restraint of tongue and pen.

Reflection: Am I willing to pray, "Bless them, change me"?

Abstinence, Sweet Abstinence

Nothing tastes as good as abstinence feels. We can choose either abstinence or disease on a daily basis. Abstinence gives us that choice. When we choose disease, choice is lost; the disease process forces us to eat addictively.

A friend says, "I remember when I had no choice but to eat. I didn't know that I had a biochemical disease—that I was addicted to certain foods. All I knew was that I had to eat."

"Then I found the food plan. With my cravings gone and a clear head, I could begin to work the Twelve Steps of a spiritual program of action. I found a loving God to guide my way. Now I have the choice of abstinence on a daily basis. I choose to follow the food plan each day, weigh and measure and eat at appropriate times. This gives me the freedom to work my program, to take care of myself for the first time in my life, and to be available to the people around me that I love so much. Abstinence is my treasure."

∽∘∾

Affirmation: I treasure the food plan exactly the way it is written.

Reflection: Am I willing to work the Twelve Step action plan?

Defiance or Reliance

We have used so much energy trying to run the show. When we came into recovery, we read in AA's *Twelve Steps and Twelve Traditions,* "No man, we saw, could believe in God and defy Him, too. Belief meant reliance, not defiance."

As we progressed in recovery, we learned that we weren't running anything. When our prayer becomes, "Show me the way," our lives will become a peaceful place. After all, doesn't God know best?

Doing it our way only brings frustration and confusion, like banging our heads against a brick wall. Complying with God's will is like floating down a gentle river. We "go with the flow." As we practice reliance on our Higher Power, we are freed from the struggle and transformed!

❧

Affirmation: *I pray only for knowledge of God's will for me and the power to carry that out.*

Reflection: *What areas of my life have I kept from God?*

Let Us Write and Reflect
on the Past Week

∽◦∾

Did I attend an adequate number of meetings?

Did I exercise too little or too much?

Did I take a Tenth Step inventory on a daily basis?

Was I accountable and honest about my food planning and implementation?

What steps did I practice?

Was I resentful, angry, selfish, dishonest or fearful?

Was I generous, kind, tolerant, patient or useful?

Were my actions, words or communications unloving or unkind?

Do I need to ask for or grant forgiveness for my actions or attitudes this week?

Was my level of hydration adequate?

Did I practice sound nutrition, including vitamins and high-quality foods?

Have I kept something to myself that should be discussed with my sponsor, advisor or therapist?

What areas of my life need improvement?

What service did I perform to help another or my group?

What was my major character flaw this week?

What was my most admirable trait this week?

Did I practice restraint of tongue and pen?

Did I rationalize any destructive behavior?

What are the corrective actions that need to be taken based on this week's inventory? Do I owe any amends?

A Program of Discovery

The tasks of recovery are less demanding than the consequences of the disease. When we come to understand this fact, we stop saying, "This recovery stuff is so hard." We no longer awfulize recovery and romanticize the disease. What we have is an exciting program of discovery!

Keeping our programs green and growing is exhilarating. We learn to grow and change without grumbling. Our worst day abstinent is better than our best day sick on sugar.

∞

Affirmation: I reap the rewards of recovery.

Reflection: Write a list of personal consequences of the disease of food addiction and list the benefits of recovery.

Sugar, Flour and Feet

"The funniest thing happened this morning. I was playing with my two-year-old son, and I grabbed his foot and pretended to eat it! I took a bite—no teeth—and pretended to chew it in my mouth. He was so upset. He said, 'Mommy, you don't eat feet, they're not on your food plan!'" From the mouths of babes come the greatest gems. That little guy hears his mom say, "I don't eat that, it's not on my food plan."

When we make a commitment to the food plan, even the babies know that we mean business. On the other hand, people sense when we are wavering too. Commitment shows, and all the power of the universe moves to make our commitment work.

Our lives show exactly what our level of commitment is: recovery or no recovery! Knowing that "half measures avail us nothing," we give our all to our program—total commitment.

୬୦୫

Affirmation: I demonstrate by my behavior that I am firm in my commitment to abstain from all addictive trigger foods.

Reflection: What are my addictive triggers, including personal binge foods?

Let Us Write and Reflect on
the Following Question

∽o∼

What can I do to have more fun in recovery?

_____

_____

_____

_____

_____

_____

_____

_____

_____

_____

_____

_____

_____

_____

_____

_____

_____

Courage Is Fear That Said Its Prayers

"The day I realized the truth of this statement, it was a turning point in my recovery. Faith means courage. I thought that courage was only granted to heroes. Then I realized that I too could choose to be courageous, especially about my food! What a concept! There wasn't a magic wand that dispensed courage to some and not to others who might be less deserving. It was my choice! It was mine all along, just like Dorothy and her ruby slippers. Now when I need to draw on my power to choose courage, I put on my ruby slippers, asking my Higher Power for help while repeating my new mantra: Courage is a choice."

Our friend who shared those words with us is a recovery hero. She has the courage to change as well as the faith that she will find the help she needs to recover from food addiction.

Courage is facing the fear and doing it anyway. Courageous change is possible when we recognize, admit and accept the fact of our addiction and then move forward despite the fear of living without our addictive food substances.

∽◦∾

Affirmation: I find the courage to change the things I can.

Reflection: What do I need to change in my life today?

Healthy Choices Support Good Recovery

We are physical, mental, emotional and spiritual beings. Healthy choices in one area are reflected in all three.

Did you ever notice how connected our emotions are with our spirit? Correcting a condition of anger or guilt that has rendered us spiritually disconnected will return us to peaceful love and acceptance.

And what about our thinking? Changing thoughts, attitudes, perceptions and beliefs are fundamental areas of concentration in our recovery process. Change a thought and the whole person changes!

Physical health affects all aspects of our lives as well. A vigorous walk feels good all over: It lifts our spirits, makes our bodies tingle and produces feelings of emotional well-being. A nap, a massage, appropriate exercise, good nutrition and adequate hydration are all good, healthy choices on the physical level.

The spiritual approach is powerful too. Prayer and meditation are healing forces with both short-term and long-term benefits. How many of us have experienced immediate relief when we gave our wills over to the care of God, performed a kind act or gave service? Spiritual practices have enormous, far-reaching results. Indeed, every healthy choice is a good recovery choice.

∽∘∾

Affirmation: I make healthy choices on a daily basis.

Reflection: Today I will make healthier choices in at least one of the following areas: fellowship, exercise, nutrition, prayer, meditation.

Let Us Write and Reflect
on the Following Idea

On awakening let us think about the twenty-four hours ahead. We consider our plans for the day. Before we begin, we ask God to direct our thinking, especially asking that it be divorced from self-pity, dishonest or self-seeking motives. When we retire at night, we constructively review our day. . . . After making our review we ask God's forgiveness and inquire what corrective measures should be taken.

Alcoholics Anonymous, p. 86

_____

_____

_____

_____

_____

_____

_____

_____

_____

_____

Let Us Write and Reflect
on the Past Week

∾∾

Did I attend an adequate number of meetings?

Did I exercise too little or too much?

Did I take a Tenth Step inventory on a daily basis?

Was I accountable and honest about my food planning and implementation?

What steps did I practice?

Was I resentful, angry, selfish, dishonest or fearful?

Was I generous, kind, tolerant, patient or useful?

Were my actions, words or communications unloving or unkind?

Do I need to ask for or grant forgiveness for my actions or attitudes this week?

Was my level of hydration adequate?

Did I practice sound nutrition, including vitamins and high-quality foods?

Have I kept something to myself that should be discussed with my sponsor, advisor or therapist?

What areas of my life need improvement?

What service did I perform to help another or my group?

What was my major character flaw this week?

What was my most admirable trait this week?

Did I practice restraint of tongue and pen?

Did I rationalize any destructive behavior?

What are the corrective actions that need to be taken based on this week's inventory? Do I owe any amends?

Automatic Thoughts

Negative automatic thoughts often sabotage our health and happiness. Automatic thoughts are generated from our old beliefs. Nothing good results from hanging on to our old ideas. We can experience no happy results until we let go of our old beliefs. That is exactly how it works. We do this one day at a time, one thought at a time, one belief at a time. Turning our old negative, destructive beliefs into affirmations takes vigilance and awareness. Toxic feelings let us know that the time has come to challenge the thoughts that create them.

With four questions, we can change our negative ideas into positive ones:

What is the feeling?

What is the thought that created the feeling?

Is that thought helpful?

What is a more helpful thought?

In recovery we identify, challenge and change the negative thoughts that create toxic feelings.

∽ᴏᴄᴠ

Affirmation: My thoughts are positive, peaceful and encouraging.

Reflection: Today I will make a list of toxic feelings, identify the negative thoughts that create them, challenge those thoughts and change them to affirming, self-enhancing thoughts.

Easy Does It

Compulsive behaviors are symptoms of addiction. Sometimes we are compelled to do a job perfectly or to get somewhere in a hurry—as if we have to do things better, sooner and bigger than anyone else.

One time I caught myself passing all my friends on the road. We were all going to the same place, and I didn't even have the key! Right then and there, I examined my compulsive need for speed. Behavior like this causes pressure and tension that puts us in danger of reaching for binge food to relieve that stress.

Part of our new way of life is "easy does it!" We need to slow down and take it easy. When we take life more slowly, we can enjoy the journey instead of fretting and stewing about the destination. Setting priorities and realistic goals, taking quiet time, and learning to act rather than react are ways to thwart compulsion and take charge of life.

࿇

Affirmation: I evaluate and correct compulsive urges to hurry, fret and react.

Reflection: How can I slow down today?

Acceptance

Acceptance is the pathway to peace. Learning to practice acceptance of situations and events of daily life will bring peace and serenity into our lives, because acceptance is the basis of a spiritual life.

Acceptance does not mean passive resignation, submission or giving up. Instead it is a rational way to face reality by taking an objective view of how things really are. The Serenity Prayer suggests that "we accept the things we cannot change." Once we understand that acceptance is a positive attitude, we can consider those things that we need to accept.

For instance, I recognize that I am a food addict by awareness of my addiction. I admit that I am a food addict by stating the fact of my addiction. I accept that I am a food addict when I give my consent—without protest!—to the fact of my food addiction. Yep, that's me: a food addict! *That* is acceptance.

Living in recovery, we learn to accept persons, places, things and situations. We give others the right to be as they choose without judging, criticizing and blaming them. After all, that is what we want for ourselves: to be accepted just the way we are today. Folks have the right to live their own lives, their way. Because we are no longer dwelling on what cannot be changed, we come to understand that happiness is not having what we want. Happiness is wanting what we have.

∾○∾

Affirmation: I accept people, places and situations just as they are today.

Reflection: What frustration am I experiencing that can be resolved by consciously accepting a person or situation?

Final Divorce

Food addicts have a romance with addictive foods. Sometimes a romance becomes disagreeable. That's what happens with food, and then the consequences of our association become unbearable. Unless we end the romance and divorce ourselves from our love, we will stay stuck in the pain and sadness of that romance gone bad.

When we come into recovery, we have to think about the divorce. We literally have to separate ourselves from what we came to think of as our best friend, our comforter! When the romance ends, we need to go about setting up a new way of life without our old love. We will experience a time of vulnerability; we may feel anger, loneliness, self-pity or depression.

The time to build a new life without our old best friend is now! The people in our helping network assist us through the period of adjustment. The tools of recovery aid us in building a new way of life that will withstand the calls from our old love. We still hear whispers in our ears: "It wasn't so bad." "You can go back for just one more bite." "Remember the joy of it." With the help of our sponsors and at meetings, we talk about these old ideas and let go absolutely, welcoming our new love: recovery!

∾o∾

Affirmation: *I surround myself with people who support my recovery.*

Reflection: *Do I entertain any thoughts which suggest that food creates comfort and love?*

Body Love

For food addicts, our bodies are often our only reality. Instead of accepting ourselves as three-dimensional—body, mind and spirit—somewhere in our addiction we begin to believe that how we look is all we are.

Some of us try to make our outsides perfect, hoping that no one will see past that to the emptiness inside. Others of us, realizing that perfection is unattainable, give up the charade completely and try to convince ourselves that our bodies have no relationship to who we are. Maybe if we can insulate ourselves behind enough layers of fat, no one can come close enough to hurt us.

No matter which way our disease outwardly manifests itself, the results are the same. No amount of food or other substance can fill that void inside. No amount of starving or purging will empty us of self-hate.

The love of God can fill us up, but we cannot grow closer to God until we are willing to treat our bodies with acceptance, love and gentleness. Our security, our sense of self-worth, and our use-fulness to God and to our fellows comes not from how we look to the world, but from where our hearts are in relation to God.

∽◦∾

Affirmation: I love and accept my body just the way it is today.

Reflection: How might I choose healing thoughts that will create and maintain my healthy body?

Surrender Is Positive

To surrender is a positive, decisive action. Surrender means letting go of something in order to gain something better. It means ending attempts to control: no more retreat and attack.

All the tactics we have tried in order to eat binge food "successfully" have failed. Most of us lost the battle against binge food a long time before we quit fighting.

A friend says, "What caused me to get into trouble with my food for the last fifteen years while sitting in recovery rooms was my lack of surrender. So what does surrender look like in me? How do I know I've surrendered? Food finally pounded me into submission. I not only lost the battle with it, but I also lost the war. I've held up my white flag; I am now willing to go to any lengths to have the merciless obsession and compulsion of addictive foods removed from me. Once I reached my bottom, I saw that I became willing to change and then developed a daily action plan to maintain a fit spiritual condition so God could and would relieve my food addiction."

The paradox is that we *surrender to win.*

∽ၜ∾

Affirmation: I peacefully acknowledge that whatever happens is supposed to happen.

Reflection: Have I surrendered all attempts to control people, places and things?

Let Us Write and Reflect
on the Past Week

ဆက

Did I attend an adequate number of meetings?

Did I exercise too little or too much?

Did I take a Tenth Step inventory on a daily basis?

Was I accountable and honest about my food planning and implementation?

What steps did I practice?

Was I resentful, angry, selfish, dishonest or fearful?

Was I generous, kind, tolerant, patient or useful?

Were my actions, words or communications unloving or unkind?

Do I need to ask for or grant forgiveness for my actions or attitudes this week?

Was my level of hydration adequate?

Did I practice sound nutrition, including vitamins and high-quality foods?

Have I kept something to myself that should be discussed with my sponsor, advisor or therapist?

What areas of my life need improvement?

What service did I perform to help another or my group?

What was my major character flaw this week?

What was my most admirable trait this week?

Did I practice restraint of tongue and pen?

Did I rationalize any destructive behavior?

What are the corrective actions that need to be taken based on this week's inventory? Do I owe any amends?

First Things First

When we come out of the fog in early recovery, we sometimes think that we have more problems than when we were in the disease. While bingeing, we temporarily forgot our problems. In abstinence, we become aware and start to face life on life's terms. Without that drug of choice—binge food—we feel edgy and vulnerable. Our challenges seem overwhelming.

How many of us have poured out our dilemma to our sponsors and heard them respond, "First things first?" That phrase really means, "Hold on, wait a minute, get your priorities straight. What is the most important thing in your life at this time?" Abstinence is first. Only after we attend to our recovery needs can we take care of that list of challenges.

The same holds true for all stages of recovery. When life gets too big, we can break it down into manageable bits and pieces. How do you eat an elephant? One bite at a time! (In four- or six-ounce servings, of course.)

In recovery, we can handle our problems one at a time. Without recovery, we can handle nothing.

∽∘∾

Affirmation: *Recovery is first!*

Reflection: *Are recovery tasks on my priority list today? Am I doing first things first?*

Today's Stress Buster:
Prepare Ahead

Abstinence requires some advanced planning. Having daily and weekly plans is a good idea. Shopping lists can be developed from menus. Having a daily to-do list helps too.

For a successful day, we plan our food, we plan our daily chores and we plan our recovery tasks.

Attainable Affirmations:
Blessings

The Irish love blessings. My bit of Irish heritage causes me to love them too. What is a blessing? A blessing is a wish or desire for good fortune for another. Today let's send good wishes to our loved ones.

An Irish blessing: May you have love that never ends, lots of money and lots of friends. Health be yours, whatever you do, and may God send many blessings to you!

∽○∾

I bless my friends and family with love and acceptance.

Feelings

People often live in fear of their feelings. In recovery we can begin to explore what various feelings mean to us. Since our feelings are messengers, we begin to view them as a part of us to be listened to, not to be feared.

Getting our feelings to work for us, we pinpoint the most current ones. After a few days of identifying our feelings, we begin to recognize them as they appear.

A friend says, "I need to immediately deal with disturbed feelings. Otherwise, I head into 'stuff-down mode,' and those feelings will never see the light of day again. They will, however, continue to surface, causing fear or anger. So much energy gets poured into holding down those stuffed feelings that could be enhancing my life. Stuffing feelings is very dangerous to my recovery, because the number-one way I stuff them is with food."

∽᠀∼

Affirmation: *I acknowledge and identify my feelings as I experience them.*

Reflection: *What feelings have surfaced today? Have I named them and claimed them?*

Humility, Not Humiliation

Humility is not humiliation. The disease was humiliating enough. Self-searching our way through the Twelve Steps brings about true humility. The Steps are a program of ego deflation at a depth. Through them we come to see ourselves as we truly are.

A longtimer in the program used to say, "Go to a corner and count yourself." Then he would go on to say, "And hope you come up with *one!*" That is our true number. We are unique and special children of God, one among many. Examining our assets and liabilities, we come to realize that we are fallible humans who have been given an opportunity to grow and change.

∽o∽

Affirmation: I enjoy the quiet peacefulness of humility.

Reflection: How do I restore myself to peace when I am blamed and despised?

Self Can't Change Self

"I can't, God can, I will let Him." In Step Two, we learn that we get our help from a higher source. Our job is to cooperate with the will of God. The unaided will alone cannot recover. The solution is simple. The solution is spiritual.

Consider the story about a man who bought a fine timepiece. He enjoyed and appreciated its precise mechanism and its beauty. When the watch needed repair, he took it to the best watchmaker in town, who was unable to fix it. The man asked, "Then what will I do to get the needed repairs?" The watch repairman said, "For a watch this fine, you must take it to its maker."

That is our answer: We return to our Maker for our necessary repair work. We are not really in "self-help" groups, we are members of "Higher Power-help" groups.

〜◦〜

Affirmation: *I go to my Maker for help and restoration.*

Reflection: *Do I work for recovery or ask for it? What are the ways I cooperate with God's plan for me?*

Let Us Write and Reflect
on the Past Week

࿙

Did I attend an adequate number of meetings?

Did I exercise too little or too much?

Did I take a Tenth Step inventory on a daily basis?

Was I accountable and honest about my food planning and implementation?

What steps did I practice?

Was I resentful, angry, selfish, dishonest or fearful?

Was I generous, kind, tolerant, patient or useful?

Were my actions, words or communications unloving or unkind?

Do I need to ask for or grant forgiveness for my actions or attitudes this week?

Was my level of hydration adequate?

Did I practice sound nutrition, including vitamins and high-quality foods?

Have I kept something to myself that should be discussed with my sponsor, advisor or therapist?

What areas of my life need improvement?

What service did I perform to help another or my group?

What was my major character flaw this week?

What was my most admirable trait this week?

Did I practice restraint of tongue and pen?

Did I rationalize any destructive behavior?

What are the corrective actions that need to be taken based on this week's inventory? Do I owe any amends?

Unconditional Abstinence

We've heard about "half measures." *The Big Book of AA* tells us that they "avail us nothing." So why settle for half measures when 100 percent abstinence results in being craving-free? The body knows when it is subjected to any amount of refined carbohydrate or other trigger foods, and the body responds with cravings.

Sometimes fear holds us back from accomplishing unconditional abstinence. We want to hold on to the illusion that we can tolerate a little of this or a little of that. Maybe we cannot imagine life without our extra bites. Until we find a sufficient substitute, we hang on to some of our old ways.

Half measures close us off to new ideas. We are convinced that our way is better. Half measures—or any program that we devise on our own—lead us to the path of relapse: a pattern of living in disease and withdrawals, going back and forth between clean abstinence and active addiction.

The answer lies in acceptance and faith. Acceptance and faith are capable of producing 100 percent abstinence. When we plan what we eat, and eat what we planned, we can achieve unconditional abstinence. We deserve a clean body and a clear head.

∽∘∾

Affirmation: I plan for and enjoy unconditional abstinence.

Reflection: Do I strictly adhere to my food plan by planning, weighing, measuring, reporting and being accountable?

God Helps Us

Sometimes I use my exercise time for prayer and affirmations.

The other day as I was walking, I was saying a prayer of supplication regarding a challenging family issue. Feeling desperate, I repeated, "God help us, God help us, God help us," with each footstep. Then the thought occurred to me to affirm God's help, so I changed my prayer to "God helps us, God helps us, God helps us." A plea for help became a powerful belief!

My spirits rose as I realized God's help is mine when I acknowledge it. The solution came almost immediately after that, a monumental gift from the universe! Thank you, God.

∽ο∾

Affirmation: God's power heals me.

Reflection: How do I practice the presence of God?

A Place of Hope

"There, within those foods that I cannot tolerate, lies my hopelessness!" Upon saying this, my friend spoke an eloquent First Step, demonstrating a firm belief that certain foods are intolerable to her.

Surely, certain foods, as well as certain attitudes and behaviors, lead us back into the hopelessness of active addiction. Permitting ourselves to take an extra bite, failing to weigh and measure, ignoring ingredient lists on labels, careless ordering in restaurants or sampling foods not on our plans—if unchecked—will take us back into disease.

Abstinence is very precise. When we manage our food according to a reliable plan, we can count on enjoying the benefits of recovery. Therein lies our hope!

∽∘∾

Affirmation: *Abstinence is my place of hope.*

Reflection: *Do I manage my food in the precise manner that my food plan indicates?*

The Refrigerator Test

"There was a lot of insanity going on in my refrigerator. The diet products were getting moldy in the back, and the high-calorie products in the front were disappearing at a rapid pace!" a friend joked.

How about all those times we had to throw out bunches of fresh vegetables because our good intentions were never realized? Those were the diet-binge days! Now, we have a plan of eating that gives us balance and boundaries.

The refrigerator will testify to our commitment to recovery. We should have some good rotation going on in there. Buying what we eat, and eating what we buy is all part of our recovery planning. We have a plan and we follow it. Shopping, preparing, reporting, committing to and executing a recovery plan keep our food in order on all levels.

∽০∾

Affirmation: I store wholesome food for a healthy body.

Reflection: Do I review the ingredients in every food I eat? Have I eliminated all foods that contain addictive substances? What changes do I need to make in order to achieve and maintain physical abstinence?

Today's Stress Buster:
Avoid Chemical Aids

*Tobacco, marijuana, alcohol, cocaine—
whether legal or illegal, these and other mind-altering
substances interfere with the body/mind's ability to
regulate its own moods. Chronic use will eventually
cause the cells to stop manufacturing "feel-good"
peptides, leading to a craving for higher
doses of the artificial stimulant.*

Candace Pert, Ph.D.

Why not do "feel-good" things from the beginning? Try sleep instead of caffeine, exercise instead of sleeping pills or yoga rather than tranquilizers. Investigate good nutrition, exercise and natural therapies as alternatives to chemical aids.

The Twelve Steps are the spiritual principles that guide us in our personal recovery. The founders of AA came up with twelve principles—Traditions—that keep our groups intact. These Twelve Traditions are to the groups what the Twelve Steps are to the individual. They are suggested principles that ensure the survival and growth of the group. Hammered out on the anvil of experience, they were designed to guide our groups. Personal survival and survival of our program depend on understanding and implementing these principles. We need to develop a personal regard for the Twelve Traditions and an awareness of our role in preserving the unity of our Twelve Step program. In recovery, we become practitioners of the Twelve Steps *and* the Twelve Traditions.

TRADITION TWO

"For our group purpose there is but one
ultimate authority—a loving God as He may
express Himself in our group conscience. Our leaders
are but trusted servants; they do not govern."

Our fellowship has only one authority: a loving God as expressed in our group conscience. Ideally, our leaders are reliable, informed, prayerful individuals who put the group's best interest first. On a personal level, we support our trusted servants. And when our time comes to serve, we do it without thought of credit or praise. Before voting in our home group, or area or regional meetings, we learn the issues and facts in order to avoid voting emotionally. We model ourselves after the "elder statesmen" described in AA's *Twelve Steps and Twelve Traditions* who "do not drive by mandate; they lead by example" (page 135).

Affirmation: I willingly support my group leaders and yield to group conscience without criticism or resentment.

Reflection: Am I an active, helpful member of my group? Do I abstain from gossip, criticism, and other divisive attitudes and behaviors?

Let Us Write and Reflect
on the Past Week

∽◦∾

Did I attend an adequate number of meetings?

Did I exercise too little or too much?

Did I take a Tenth Step inventory on a daily basis?

Was I accountable and honest about my food planning and implementation?

What steps did I practice?

Was I resentful, angry, selfish, dishonest or fearful?

Was I generous, kind, tolerant, patient or useful?

Were my actions, words or communications unloving or unkind?

Do I need to ask for or grant forgiveness for my actions or attitudes this week?

Was my level of hydration adequate?

Did I practice sound nutrition, including vitamins and high-quality foods?

Have I kept something to myself that should be discussed with my sponsor, advisor or therapist?

What areas of my life need improvement?

What service did I perform to help another or my group?

What was my major character flaw this week?

What was my most admirable trait this week?

Did I practice restraint of tongue and pen?

Did I rationalize any destructive behavior?

What are the corrective actions that need to be taken based on this week's inventory? Do I owe any amends?

Bet Your Life

Faith is comprised of belief and trust. "Belief" is intellectual and means agreeing to the truth of something offered for acceptance. "Trust" is acting on that belief.

A great tightrope walker once walked over Niagara Falls with a wheelbarrow. Then he asked a little boy if he thought the tightrope walker could balance the little boy in the wheelbarrow and take him for a ride across the falls. The little boy was sure he could. Next the performer asked the child to hop into the wheelbarrow for a ride. The boy ran and hid behind his mother. The youngster believed, but he did not trust; he did not have faith enough to take the ride. He wouldn't bet his life on it.

Faith without trust goes nowhere. Faith implies certainty—a willingness to bet our lives on the outcome. A funny old saying in recovery circles is that "I would rather go through life abstinent, believing I am a food addict, than go through life addicted, trying to convince myself that I am not." When we follow our Twelve Step program, we place our faith in abstinence and in the power of God to release us from the control of addictive foods. We bet our lives on it!

∽∘∾

Affirmation: I trust my food plan. It is just right for me.

Reflection: Am I willing to bet my life and my health on my food choices?

44

Not Guilty!

Cervantes said, "No man's born wise." How many times have we been found guilty by ourselves or others because we had not acted wisely? As children we were not told the rules and yet were expected to keep them. Throughout our lives, we felt ashamed or embarrassed because we acted in a certain way, although we had no idea of how to behave at all in a given circumstance. Life is truly a trial-and-error proposition.

Where did our guidelines come from? Who followed the rules? We were told not to scream or yell by people who screamed and yelled. Childhood—really, all of life—is confusing, and we often spend years sorting out what works for us. Wisdom comes from experience.

Addicts in recovery are lucky. We find twelve guidelines for a disorder that backs us into such a tight corner that we become willing to follow them. When we enter the program, we start in the kindergarten of life and gain experience while living according to a new set of principles. Doing the steps, we learn to evaluate and correct our attitudes and behaviors. The inventory and amends steps allow us to clean up the guilt and remorse connected to those we harmed in the past. As we persevere in the recovery process, we build our character. We find what we have been searching for: a set of principles to guide our lives, connect us with others and show us the way to God.

∞◦∞

Affirmation: *The Twelve Steps guide my spiritual growth.*

Reflection: *What step am I working on today?*

Today Is Love Day

We can look at love in many ways. An academic would tell us about different types of love: *agape, eros, phileo*—respectively, unconditional love, romantic love and the affection of friends for each other. Most of us have experienced all of these, yet none exactly describes the state of love.

Love is a state of being to be strived for and desired. It is a place to live! It does not involve a single object of love. It is the love that exists in the world of the Spirit. We can live in that place of love only when we become free of the negative reactions of anger, fear, hurt and pain, and the conditions that cause them.

Being *in love* does not mean being gaga over a particular person. It means being in a state free from judgment, criticism, blame, expectations, assumptions and other thought processes that bring misery to ourselves and others. That type of love—where we strive to be—is where God lives. It is heaven! We won't be there all the time, but the Twelve Steps show us how to return when we stray from love.

∽○∽

Affirmation: I am free to love.

Reflection: Am I willing to give up judgment, criticism, blame, expectations and assumptions in order to be in a place of love?

Long Lines Lead to Long Lives

I take offense at being kept waiting—for anything. My friend doesn't mind waiting in long lines; in fact, he just loves to be kept waiting. He believes that for every minute he waits, his life will be extended an equal number of minutes. In his view, impatience shortens life while patience has the opposite effect.

When we take offense at what life offers, we create a toxic environment for ourselves and others. We snap, we snarl, we growl and we create a poisoned atmosphere. Virginia Satir said, "It is not so much what happens but how we handle it that makes all the difference. Problems are not the problem; coping is the problem." How we cope with the world as we find it makes the difference between war and peace. How then shall we cope? Most of what we fuss about isn't worth the bother. A line never moved faster because we complained.

The whole problem about waiting is our attitude. Attitudes can be changed. From now on, let's have the new attitude that lines are a terrific opportunity to extend our lives. A change of attitude creates acceptance, and acceptance brings peace. We learn to live life on life's terms.

✧

Affirmation: I identify my negative thoughts and change them to positive ones.

Reflection: What is my attitude about being kept waiting?

Building a Life of Recovery

We build a program that will get us abstinent and keep us abstinent. Step work, getting a sponsor, praying and meditating, attending meetings, reading the literature, adhering to a food plan and making phone calls are the recommended practices of a good recovery program. Healthy choices such as good nutrition, reasonable exercise, adequate rest and hydration contribute to our sense of well-being and strengthen recovery. These elements define the *recovery process.*

During this process, another one may occur that is called the *relapse process.* The relapse process involves the gradual erosion of effective practices, accompanied by the return of symptoms of the disease. The critical recovery tool that aids us in recognizing this phenomenon is our daily checklist. Each day, we must know in which direction we are headed. We ask ourselves, "Where am I going today: toward recovery or disease?" We work to strengthen our program and catch ourselves when we spot weaknesses.

An honest evening inventory helps identify weak places in our program. This gives us a good chance of avoiding relapse. We build a healthy life, one recovery task at a time.

∽◦∾

Affirmation: *Each day, I spot, admit and correct flaws in my recovery program.*

Reflection: *Do I carefully review my recovery program in order to ensure that it is adequate to support continuing abstinence?*

Let Us Write and Reflect on
the Following Question

∽∘∾

What is my conscience saying that I am ignoring?

_____

_____

_____

_____

_____

_____

_____

_____

_____

_____

_____

_____

_____

_____

_____

_____

_____

Let Us Write and Reflect
on the Past Week

∽◦∾

Did I attend an adequate number of meetings?

Did I exercise too little or too much?

Did I take a Tenth Step inventory on a daily basis?

Was I accountable and honest about my food planning and implementation?

What steps did I practice?

Was I resentful, angry, selfish, dishonest or fearful?

Was I generous, kind, tolerant, patient or useful?

Were my actions, words or communications unloving or unkind?

Do I need to ask for or grant forgiveness for my actions or attitudes this week?

Was my level of hydration adequate?

Did I practice sound nutrition, including vitamins and high-quality foods?

Have I kept something to myself that should be discussed with my sponsor, advisor or therapist?

What areas of my life need improvement?

What service did I perform to help another or my group?

What was my major character flaw this week?

What was my most admirable trait this week?

Did I practice restraint of tongue and pen?

Did I rationalize any destructive behavior?

What are the corrective actions that need to be taken based on this week's inventory? Do I owe any amends?

A Conversation with Both of Me

The addict's credo is that if a little is good, more is better. That idea may lurk in our lower consciousness forever.

Recently, after finishing my evening dairy and fruit, a thought floated up: "It would be nice to have more fruit." So my recovering self said, "Why?" My addictive self said, "It would be more satisfying." "Aha!" said my recovering self. "More fruit is not more satisfying. It will open the door for more, then more, and more and more than that. There will be no end to it. Having more will not be satisfying. There is no satisfaction there. The real satisfaction lies in the safety of the food plan, just the way it is written. No more, no less!"

The longer we are abstinent, the more we see how the slightest deviation from the food plan will set up mental obsession first and then physical craving. When we achieve abstinence from the addictive substances of sugar, flour and wheat, we can have "the second thought" when those cunning thoughts return. Let's make the second thought one of a positive, healing recovery!

∽o∽

Affirmation: I deserve abstinence, growth and the gifts of recovery.

Reflection: How do I handle it when I think about deviating from the food plan?

Let Us Write and Reflect
on the Following Idea

When we are abstinent from the addictive substances of sugar, flour and wheat, we can have "the second thought" if the mental obsession returns.

Recovery from Food Addiction, Inc., Abstinence Guidelines

The Telephone in Our Tool Kit

It all started with a phone call. The most important phone call ever made by a recovering alcoholic in search of support was the one that led to Bill W. and Dr. Bob's first meeting. In a split second in the Mayflower Hotel, as Bill turned away from the bar and toward the telephone directory, lives were saved.

Are the phone calls we make any less important? I think not. Our phone calls are lifesaving too! Often we hear recovering people say, "A phone call came when I most needed it."

Collecting phone numbers from the "we care" phone lists that are passed around at recovery meetings is often an addict's first step to recovery. Little address books are our first line of defense against the disease of addiction. Addicts never need to recover in isolation. The phone puts us in touch with recovering people nearby and far away.

∽∘∾

Affirmation: *I reach out to give and get support and encouragement.*

Reflection: *Do I make at least three phone calls a day to maintain contact with other people in recovery?*

A Recovery Plan

We create a daily plan that states our goals. We are accountable when we report this plan to our sponsor. In the evening, we review this plan to determine if we have met our goals.

A friend shares her daily plan:

- Plan and commit my food.
- Eat what I commit or report every change.
- Pray first thing in the morning, last thing at night and as needed.
- Talk with my sponsor.
- Talk to other food addicts on the phone.
- Drink at least a gallon of water.
- Take vitamins.
- Do a Tenth Step, journal and gratitude list, and e-mail it to my sponsor.
- Meditate twice.
- Exercise for forty-five minutes.
- Read a meditation.

She says, "The list is long, and I am not perfect. I catch the areas that need attention when I do my Tenth Step and evaluate and correct. In other words, I make an action plan that I include in my journaling, so I am not saying, 'Oh well, I have not had enough water. I will drink more tomorrow.' Rather I plan to carry a gallon jug so it is easier to track what I drink.

"A lot of recovery behaviors keep me from playing with the food plan each day. When those behaviors have a place in my daily life, they form the structure around which I plan my day.

"I get a lot of living in as well. I am a food addict. I know it and surrender to that fact. I also know that there is a way that I can live that is not controlled by food. I can have a daily reprieve. It is a much easier, softer way of life than I ever lived before. It is a life in which I don't have to hate myself."

∽○∽

Affirmation: I choose a workable recovery plan.

Reflection: Do I have a plan that keeps me in strong recovery?

Cave Dwelling

When she describes her tendency to isolate, my friend says, "I have an emotional cave that I crawl into."

Isolation, whatever form it takes, is a vital factor in addictive disease and relapse. Isolation usually entails avoiding phone calls, meetings and other human contacts in the recovery community.

As we isolate, our recovery slogan changes into a relapse mantra. "Stick with the winners" becomes "Avoid the winners." This path is risky because we deny ourselves the support that our helping network can provide.

The tendency to isolate is pervasive in addicts. We learned how to isolate when we were in active addiction, and these secretive ways follow us into recovery.

By overcoming isolation and concealment, we become involved in our recovery community, finding true intimacy with sponsors and recovery buddies where there is great power to be found. We are not alone there.

That the first word of our Twelve Steps is "we" is no mistake. Together we can do what we could never do by ourselves.

∽૦∾

Affirmation: I keep the lines of communication open with my recovery support network.

Reflection: What happens when I isolate?

Glory the Gory Days

Food addicts have selective memories! Sometimes we experience memories of the "good old days" and the exhilaration of eating favorite dishes and baked goods. These memories of the pleasurable feelings produced by the addictive substances are referred to as "euphoric recall." Because the release of brain chemicals affects the pleasure centers of the brain, addicts experience pleasurable feelings after ingesting addictive substances.

Memories of the "high" become a compelling part of the addictive process. We think fondly of those times when we were lost in addictive disease, believing we ate to feel better. The truth is we always felt worse. Addiction results in short-term pleasure and lasting pain.

On the other hand, in recovery that sequence is reversed. We experience short-term pain followed by real pleasure. The short-term pain of withdrawals is our investment in the enduring rewards of recovery.

Remember that every person who is enjoying recovery has worked through the emotional, physical and spiritual challenges of the early days. There is no way around it. The only way through it is through it! No matter what the challenges of life are in recovery, the worst day abstinent is better than the best day in disease.

∽∘∾

Affirmation: *Abstinent recovery is the healthy, happy way for me.*

Reflection: *I will make a list of the consequences of food addiction in order to dispel the mistaken belief that binge food makes life better.*

Let Us Write and Reflect
on the Past Week

༄

Did I attend an adequate number of meetings?

Did I exercise too little or too much?

Did I take a Tenth Step inventory on a daily basis?

Was I accountable and honest about my food planning and implementation?

What steps did I practice?

Was I resentful, angry, selfish, dishonest or fearful?

Was I generous, kind, tolerant, patient or useful?

Were my actions, words or communications unloving or unkind?

Do I need to ask for or grant forgiveness for my actions or attitudes this week?

Was my level of hydration adequate?

Did I practice sound nutrition, including vitamins and high-quality foods?

Have I kept something to myself that should be discussed with my sponsor, advisor or therapist?

What areas of my life need improvement?

What service did I perform to help another or my group?

What was my major character flaw this week?

What was my most admirable trait this week?

Did I practice restraint of tongue and pen?

Did I rationalize any destructive behavior?

What are the corrective actions that need to be taken based on this week's inventory? Do I owe any amends?

What Other People Think Is None of My Business

After experiencing a substantial weight gain, my client met an old friend. She said, "I know what he was thinking and I felt so ashamed!" *Wrong!* She could *guess* what he was thinking; she could *ask* what he was thinking; she could *presume to know* what he was thinking; but she did not *know* what he was thinking. She projected her own thoughts onto him.

Sometimes we honestly believe that we know what others think. The problem is that we create thoughts based on our assumptions about what someone else is thinking, and then we react emotionally to what we think they think. The whole process is fiction!

Adults stuck in addiction are like young children who are egocentric and don't realize that others have a different point of view. Because we all interpret things differently according to our own experiences, we cannot know another's thoughts. We lack mind-reading capabilities. Actually, the only mind we can read is our own.

The path to another's point of view is through communication. Investigation and communication provide the way to overcome separation and connect with others in a meaningful way. Communication is the means for getting out of self and growing beyond our own perceptions. Only with communication can we form relationships based upon genuine understanding.

∽○∾

Affirmation: I think peaceful thoughts.

Reflection: Do I strive to understand another person's point of view by using good communication skills? Do I make assumptions or check things out?

Eating Addictively Will Always Make Everything Worse

For a long time in the process of eating addictively, we believed that we were having a good time, that food was our friend—a comforter. We loved to eat because eating produced a drugged state that we confused with peace. Of course, we couldn't hold on to that feeling. It was followed by a state of sluggishness—the price of the drugged state.

Our lives went out of control along with our eating. We ate everything in sight no matter what the consequences. Then we decided to change our lives—not because we wanted to give up our food-induced fog, but because we wanted to look or feel or be better! In recovery, we begin to recognize the insanity of our old actions.

In the process of working the Twelve Steps, we came to understand our irrational relationship with food. Once in the program, we fully concede our food addiction to our innermost selves. The important issue is for us to stay convinced of the danger of addictive foods, to watchfully reject the ideas of food as a comforter or friend. For this action, we need a plan. We need to keep our memory green, remembering the consequences of addiction. Before the *next* binge, we want to remember the negative outcomes of our *last* binge.

∽०∽

Affirmation: *I value abstinence as the genuine path to peace of mind.*

Reflection: *Today I will review and list the ways my life became unmanageable in addiction.*

Attainable Affirmations:
Life Is Now

We are safe in the moment. Fear is projecting thoughts into the future. Guilt is meddling with the past. Because we can neither change the past nor live in the future, this here-and-now moment is the place where life happens and safety reigns. The present is the point of all power.

∽∘∽

I am safe in the moment, right here, right now.

Serenity

God, grant me the serenity
to accept the things I cannot change,
courage to change the things I can and
the wisdom to know the difference.

Reinhold Niebuhr

The Serenity Prayer is a very practical, clear-cut set of instructions. It instructs us to ask God for serenity, acceptance and courage. First we ask for the serenity to accept those things we cannot change. Then we ask for the wisdom to know what to do and the courage to do it. Learning what to change comes from listening to recovering people, our sponsors, spiritual advisors and others who have overcome our kind of challenges. From them, we learn to identify the changeable versus the unchangeable.

Our bodies act as the limit that sets our boundaries. Everything outside our bodies is unchangeable. That is what we accept. Everything inside our bodies—what we think, what we say and what we do—can be changed. Certainly courage is needed to change the things we can—ourselves!

Distinguishing what we can change and what we cannot is comforting. We no longer try to change the world. We come to see that the world around us changes when we change ourselves.

∽⚬∾

Affirmation: *God grants me the serenity to accept the things I cannot change. God grants me the courage to change the things I can. God grants me the wisdom to know the difference.*

Reflection: *What does the Serenity Prayer mean to me?*

Squeaky-Clean Abstinence

How do we know if we have achieved clean abstinence? One of the yardsticks to measure abstinence is freedom from cravings, compulsions and obsessions.

Physical cravings result from the ingestion of addictive substances. They are physical urges caused by the presence of addictive trigger food and the subsequent withdrawal from them. Compulsions are repetitive behaviors such as automatic eating achieved without conscious thought or effort. Obsession is mental. Obsessions are persistent intrusive thoughts. We may experience obsessions in the absence of addictive trigger foods—thinking obsessively about binge food, despite good physical abstinence. Mental "sobriety" involves taking charge of obsessive thinking—changing our thoughts from "food thoughts" to "recovery thoughts."

The disease process is filled with cravings, compulsions and obsessions. In recovery, we experience relief from them. First the cravings go when we achieve "squeaky-clean" abstinence. When we have good food management, compulsive eating behavior is resolved. Obsessions are addressed by daily vigilance. We become aware of our obsessive thoughts of food and weight. After all, they are just thoughts, and thoughts can be changed.

∽o∾

Affirmation: I choose thoughts and behaviors consistent with recovery.

Reflection: Have I been experiencing intrusive, obsessive thoughts about food? Do I continue to eat compulsively? What are the remedies for obsession and compulsion?

Learning to Identify, Not Compare

When we make a firm commitment to recovery, we concentrate on identifying with what we hear at meetings. When we are not so committed, we are more apt to make comparisons: "That's not my style." "I didn't do that!"

When we identify, we feel that we are in the right place. When we compare, we seem out of our element. We don't belong.

In the program we learn to identify, not compare, so that we can reach out to those with whom we share common ground. Looking at our differences puts up barriers to recovery—identification tears them down. No matter how we behaved in addiction, we see that we share the same attitudes, feelings and character defects. We learn to identify, not compare.

Identification as food addicts allows us to focus on our similarities, not our differences. This action ends isolation as we become part of the positive process of recovery.

కింు

Affirmation: I identify positively with other recovering food addicts.

Reflection: Do I identify or compare? At meetings, do I look for ideas that will help me in my recovery?

Made a Decision

When we hit bottom emotionally, we are ready for Step Three. We called out to our Higher Power, "Take me and change me, I cannot go on like this."

Notice how the Second Step brings us to the place where we desire sanity. It opens the door to this decision to choose something more peaceful than the lunacy of our lives in addiction. In this action step we decide to transfer our power to a better caretaker. Our behavior changes because we have a new Director.

> *We decided that hereafter in this drama of life, God was going to be our Director. He is the principal; we are His agents. He is the Father, and we are His children. . . . This concept was the keystone of the new and triumphant arch through which we passed to freedom.*

Alcoholics Anonymous, p. 62

౷౦౷

Affirmation: *I affirm my decision to turn my life and my will over to the care of God as I understand him.*

Reflection: *What willful choices do I cling to?*

Let Us Write and Reflect
on the Past Week

∽∾∾

Did I attend an adequate number of meetings?

Did I exercise too little or too much?

Did I take a Tenth Step inventory on a daily basis?

Was I accountable and honest about my food planning and implementation?

What steps did I practice?

Was I resentful, angry, selfish, dishonest or fearful?

Was I generous, kind, tolerant, patient or useful?

Were my actions, words or communications unloving or unkind?

Do I need to ask for or grant forgiveness for my actions or attitudes this week?

Was my level of hydration adequate?

Did I practice sound nutrition, including vitamins and high-quality foods?

Have I kept something to myself that should be discussed with my sponsor, advisor or therapist?

What areas of my life need improvement?

What service did I perform to help another or my group?

What was my major character flaw this week?

What was my most admirable trait this week?

Did I practice restraint of tongue and pen?

Did I rationalize any destructive behavior?

What are the corrective actions that need to be taken based on this week's inventory? Do I owe any amends?

Relapse Is Not an Event

Sometimes we think about relapse as taking place at that exact moment when we return to eating addictive foods. Actually, relapse is a process that precedes that first bite.

Relapse is a series of events that contribute to the breakdown of our recovery process and that lead us back into the disease. In a way, relapse is like throwing away the recovery tools that we use to establish and maintain recovery.

The good news is that—with close scrutiny—we can identify our relapse indicators, learn to understand our patterns of relapse and intervene when we start down that path. Taking an inventory of the weaknesses in my recovery program helps me to identify my relapse warning signs. Then I can pinpoint the strengths that lead me away from relapse.

∽✤∾

Affirmation: *I maintain recovery by identifying dangerous behaviors and patterns.*

Reflection: *Do I regularly identify behaviors that weaken my recovery? Starting today, I will list my relapse warning signs.*

Let's Write and Reflect on
the Following Idea

∽o∽

If you are not in the process of recovery, you are in the process of relapse. Recovery is like going up a down escalator. There is no such thing as standing still; as soon as you stop going up you begin moving backwards.

Miller, Gorski and Miller, *Learning to Live Again,* p. 208

_____

_____

_____

_____

_____

_____

_____

_____

_____

_____

_____

_____

_____

Don't Worry, Be Happy

My friend sends me recovery thoughts. One of his favorites is: "If there is something that you can do about it, then why worry? If there is nothing that you can do about it, then why worry?" Let's look at the logic of that idea.

Worry is such a waste of time. Worry thoughts create fear—a discomforting emotion. One of the most effective things we can do to work on our troubling thoughts is to ask ourselves, "Is this thought helpful?" If it is not helpful, then why not change the thought into one that is beneficial? Since what we focus on increases, let's focus on safety, security, abundance and peace instead of want, lack, trouble and difficulties.

Changing our troubling thoughts into affirming ones takes work. However, that kind of effort pays off when peace replaces fear. According to the philosopher Ovid, "Happy the man who has broken the chains which hurt the mind, and has given up worrying, once and for all."

∽⌒∽

Affirmation: I change troublesome thoughts to helpful ideas.

Reflection: How much time do I spend worrying? What tools do I use to change anxious thoughts to secure thoughts?

Two Wolves

A Native American grandfather was talking to his grandson about how he felt. He said, "I feel as if I have two wolves fighting in my heart. One wolf is the vengeful, angry, violent one. The other wolf is the loving, compassionate one."

The grandson asked him, "Which wolf will win the fight in your heart?"

The grandfather answered: "The one I feed."

Which shall I feed today?

∽⊙∾

Affirmation: *I practice the spiritual principles of love and compassion.*

Reflection: *How do I feed my angry self? In what ways can I enhance my compassionate self?*

Today's Stress Buster:
Write It Down

Things We Write Down and Why

Goals: Writing puts the process in motion and allows for frequent reviews and revision when necessary. Abstinence opens the door to new goals and visions.

Journal writing: A good way to get to know personal motivations, inner wisdom, blocks to progress, hidden feelings and ideas. Even step work goes into our journal.

Dreams: When you remember a dream, write it down. Then look for the message in it. It is nice to notice when in recovery the nightmares stop.

Food and exercise plans: The best way to make a commitment to healthy choices is to write them down as a written contract. The written word is more concrete.

Phone messages, notes and reminders: Write them down and remember where you put them.

To-do list: A written daily plan of action clarifies and simplifies the day.

The Twelve Steps are the spiritual principles that guide us in our personal recovery. The founders of AA came up with twelve principles—Traditions—that keep our groups intact. These Twelve Traditions are to the groups what the Twelve Steps are to the individual. They are suggested principles that ensure the survival and growth of the group. Hammered out on the anvil of experience, they were designed to guide our groups. Personal survival and survival of our program depend on understanding and implementing these principles. We need to develop a personal regard for the Twelve Traditions and an awareness of our role in preserving the unity of our Twelve Step program. In recovery, we become practitioners of the Twelve Steps *and* the Twelve Traditions.

TRADITION THREE

*"The only requirement for membership is the
desire to stop eating addictively."*

Our fellowships are not social clubs. There are no membership rules. We are members if we say so.

One time I was invited and then uninvited to speak at a convention. The reason given was that "you are not a member." One of their members joked, "Did you forget to send in your membership application?"

Actually, programs based upon the Twelve Traditions are inclusive, never exclusive. The doors are open to every food addict/ compulsive overeater. No membership applications required! There are no barriers between the suffering addict and the program that will save his/her life.

On a personal level, we need to guard against setting up any obstacles against any food addict who wishes to participate in our Twelve Step way of life. We need never let our biases interfere with our ability to carry the message. No one is too sick, too strange, too different to be barred from our lifesaving programs of recovery.

∽o∾

Affirmation: I welcome anyone who wishes to attend our meetings. I take my own inventory only.

Reflection: Do I carefully refrain from exhibiting prejudice against food addicts who wish to be part of my recovery group? How do I correct such prejudices and biases?

Let Us Write and Reflect
on the Past Week

ঔৡ

Did I attend an adequate number of meetings?

Did I exercise too little or too much?

Did I take a Tenth Step inventory on a daily basis?

Was I accountable and honest about my food planning and implementation?

What steps did I practice?

Was I resentful, angry, selfish, dishonest or fearful?

Was I generous, kind, tolerant, patient or useful?

Were my actions, words or communications unloving or unkind?

Do I need to ask for or grant forgiveness for my actions or attitudes this week?

Was my level of hydration adequate?

Did I practice sound nutrition, including vitamins and high-quality foods?

Have I kept something to myself that should be discussed with my sponsor, advisor or therapist?

What areas of my life need improvement?

What service did I perform to help another or my group?

What was my major character flaw this week?

What was my most admirable trait this week?

Did I practice restraint of tongue and pen?

Did I rationalize any destructive behavior?

What are the corrective actions that need to be taken based on this week's inventory? Do I owe any amends?

Let the Attitude Be Gratitude

"Ask, and it shall be given you;
seek, and you shall find; knock, and it shall be
opened unto you: For everyone that asks receives;
and he that seeks finds; and to him that
knocks, it shall be opened."

Matthew 7:7-8

We always get what we seek.

When we look at life gratefully, life looks so good to us. The opposite is also true. When we look at life critically, it doesn't look so great.

We can look at people that way too, by looking through our grateful glasses or our critical ones. We truly do find what we seek.

Keeping a list of the things we are grateful for creates a positive focus. When we are having a bad day, we can look back with gratitude when we count our blessings instead of our troubles. We deserve to see the good in life.

ༀ

Affirmation: I look at the world with grateful eyes.

Reflection: Today I will list and reflect on ten things for which I am thankful.

The Flip Side to Forgiveness Is Resentment

The spiritual world and the material world are so different. Let's look at the idea of forgiveness.

The world's idea is to let the offender off the hook—to grant a pardon. The spiritual way of forgiveness is to let ourselves off the hook.

We move into a position of unforgiveness by judging others. We deem them to be bad or wrongdoers. When judging, we create our own victimhood. We are the real victims of the anger, rage and resentment created by the judgment. Toxic anger grows into resentment and rage. It's like drinking poison and expecting the other person to die.

Forgiveness is an exquisite spiritual process that involves suspending judgment. By releasing our need to be right and to find fault, we find our way to love and acceptance of the person we have judged and condemned. Moving from condemnation to love and acceptance by following the path of forgiveness, we become filled with peaceful feelings.

∽∘∾

Affirmation: I love and accept you just the way you are today because love and acceptance are spiritual principles and I choose to live a spiritual way of life. I choose love!

Reflection: Today I will identify a resentment and return to a place of love with that person.

Getting on the Love Train

It may be a good idea to get into a loving space before going out into the world in the morning. That's what I did recently when I knew I would be meeting someone who had verbally lashed out at me in the past. I inhaled the feeling of love. When I started to weaken, I was able to get back into a strong loving place each time. The bottom line was that there were no instances of his acting out. He was great!

Recently when I was with someone else, I decided to do the same thing. Usually I start out fine with this person who visits for several days, then I start to notice irritating things. Sometimes I pick-pick-pick (mentally) at her until I get irritable and glad to see her leave. This time I stayed in the love mode and enjoyed being with her from arrival until departure. This is really practicing the principles of Step Twelve.

Love is such a great and peaceful principle.

∾∞∾

Affirmation: I consciously practice love and enjoy the peace and power it creates.

Reflection: What attitudes and behaviors keep me in an unloving place? How can I change these to loving ones?

Personal Responsibility for Personal Binge Foods

Our recovery is based upon abstinence from all addictive foods and behaviors, including personal binge foods and volume, plus commitment to a weighed and measured food plan.

Our food plans may list a food that is a problem for us. What a struggle that can be. After all, the food plan "allows" for that food. We "should" be able to handle it!

Here we become personally responsible for our abstinence by eliminating a personal binge food. We read the signals from our bodies and choose clean abstinence. We ask ourselves, "Are there problem foods that need to be eliminated from my food plan?" The next step is to get rid of them! We remove them from the cupboard, take them off the grocery list and make a firm commitment to abstain from them permanently. Then we speak to our sponsors about this decision so that we become accountable for our abstinence from this personal binge food.

༺૦૭

Affirmation: *I am honest in my use of all foods.*

Reflection: *Do I review my relationship with personal binge foods in order to identify and eliminate them?*

Gossip

A Chasidic tale illustrates a point about gossip: A man went about the community telling malicious lies about the rabbi. Later, he realized the wrong he had done and began to feel remorse. He went to the rabbi and begged his forgiveness, saying he would do anything he could to make amends. The rabbi told the man, "Take a feather pillow, cut it open and scatter the feathers to the winds." The man thought this was a strange request, but it was a simple enough task, and he did it gladly. When he returned to tell the rabbi that he had done it, the rabbi said, "Now, go and gather the feathers. Because you can no more make amends for the damage your words have done than you can recollect the feathers."

A friend shares, "I listened to some gossip that I thought would help me make a proper decision. It made things worse and I had nightmares. I feel awful for listening and opening my mouth in what I call justified gossiping. I will work on this today with the help of my Higher Power."

We cannot predict the harm done by gossip. When our words go out into the world, we have no way of taking them back. Better to say nothing about another person, whether positive or negative, true or untrue. Better not to listen to tales about others too.

∽∘∾

Affirmation: *My words are thoughtful and kind.*

Reflection: *Am I willing to identify one thing I can do to eliminate gossip in my life today?*

Let Us Write and Reflect on
the Following Question

༺๏๏

What are the obstacles that keep me from achieving balance in my life?

_____

_____

_____

_____

_____

_____

_____

_____

_____

_____

_____

_____

_____

_____

_____

Let Us Write and Reflect
on the Past Week

∽◦∾

Did I attend an adequate number of meetings?

Did I exercise too little or too much?

Did I take a Tenth Step inventory on a daily basis?

Was I accountable and honest about my food planning and implementation?

What steps did I practice?

Was I resentful, angry, selfish, dishonest or fearful?

Was I generous, kind, tolerant, patient or useful?

Were my actions, words or communications unloving or unkind?

Do I need to ask for or grant forgiveness for my actions or attitudes this week?

Was my level of hydration adequate?

Did I practice sound nutrition, including vitamins and high-quality foods?

Have I kept something to myself that should be discussed with my sponsor, advisor or therapist?

What areas of my life need improvement?

What service did I perform to help another or my group?

What was my major character flaw this week?

What was my most admirable trait this week?

Did I practice restraint of tongue and pen?

Did I rationalize any destructive behavior?

What are the corrective actions that need to be taken based on this week's inventory? Do I owe any amends?

What Is My Intention?
Where Is My Attention?

Change is brought about by two qualities: attention and intention. If our lifelong plan is to grow, then we need to know that intention is so powerful that when we put forth our intention to recover, our recovery is assured. Each day we renew and reaffirm this intention. From it springs the willingness to pay attention to the recovery principles that are needed to stay on our chosen path.

So often we have seen individuals start out strong with obvious plans to recover. They attend meetings, report food plans, pray, meditate, read the literature and make phone calls. Usually they recognize and praise the benefits of recovery. Then by the hundreds we see them fall away as their intention wavers and their attention turns to family, work, school and even religious pursuits. Fewer meetings and contacts with recovery become no meetings or contacts with recovery. When warned of the possibility of relapse, they argue, debate or attack. We watch helplessly as their programs disintegrate and disappear.

Something can be learned from each and every relapse.

∽○∽

Affirmation: *I intend to stay abstinent, trust God, clean house and be of service to others.*

Reflection: *Am I going forward in recovery or backward toward relapse? What can I do to assure that I will continue to go forward?*

Let Us Write and Reflect
on the Following Idea

We have to grow or else deteriorate. For us, the status quo can only be for today, never for tomorrow. Change we must; we cannot stand still.

A.A. Grapevine

Faith Is a Lighted Doorway.
Trust Is a Dark Hall

Does God really know what is best? The phone rings and the news is horrible. We are plunged into shock and darkness beyond imagining. Here is our worst nightmare. We drop to our knees to ask for help and we are told "Trust God."

Then we take a step down that dark hallway of trusting and letting go. It happens slowly. We come out of the shock gradually; it might take months. Driving by a church marquee, we see the message reads, "If you pray, why worry? If you worry, why pray?" This comment brings a smile to our lips. We realize that we are surviving and finding answers.

The day comes when we *know* that God takes all things and transcends them for our greatest spiritual good.

❦

Affirmation: God is my refuge, my power, my strength. In the world of the spirit, I am safe, secure and protected.

Reflection: Do I trust God to take my pain and transform it to my greatest good? How do I become more trusting?

I Choose Healthy Ways to Create Good Feelings

Addicts obsessively pursue feeling good . . . no matter how bad it makes us feel. It's irrational but that is the course of addiction. When we use our drug of choice, we get a fifteen-minute lift from it. However, what goes up, must come down.

Because our body and brain have been flooded with the addictive substance—refined and processed foods—the body recognizes that it is in crisis. The pancreas releases insulin, which starts grabbing sugar from the bloodstream, thus depleting the brain and body of needed sugar and creating a twenty-four-hour withdrawal crisis. What do we do next? We compulsively take larger doses more often, creating greater and more frequent crises. Each crisis takes us lower physically, emotionally and spiritually. The cycle is a no-win situation, and yet we go on believing that we eat to feel better.

So here's the math: we pay for a fifteen-minute high with twenty-four hours of pain. In recovery, we find healthy ways to produce good feelings.

∾∘∾

Affirmation: *I go to my Higher Power to release me from the destructive power of food addiction.*

Reflection: *Do I recognize and admit that active food addiction places me in the grip of a destructive power greater than myself? Have I gone to my Higher Power to relieve me from that destructive force?*

The Wisdom Prayer

This slightly rewritten Serenity Prayer is a good tool to keep us from fooling ourselves:

> *God grant me the serenity to accept the person I cannot change, courage to change the person I can, and the wisdom to know that that person is me!*

There is power in those words. When we recognize that we cannot change the world or anybody in it, we see that the only one we can change is ourselves. The inner world where our thoughts, actions and words originate can be changed. The outside world is subject to acceptance. We can save time and energy by understanding and applying that principle.

∽∘∾

Affirmation: *I align my thoughts, words and deeds with recovery principles.*

Reflection: *Do I identify what needs to be changed in me? Have I humbly asked God to remove these shortcomings? Do I make a conscious attempt to apply the principles of the Twelve Steps?*

Sponsorship

When you hang on to your sponsor with one hand and a new person with your other hand, which one would you use to binge?

From the AA preamble, we learn that we are involved in "a fellowship of men and women who share their experience, strength and hope with each other that they may solve their common problem and help others to recover."

Being involved with others in the program keeps us focused on recovery. A sponsor is one to turn to for guidance and help. When we sponsor others, we get out of ourselves. Since sharing is the best form of learning, usually those ideas we share with those we sponsor are exactly what we need to hear. Sponsoring a newcomer to recovery keeps our memory green.

∽∘∾

Affirmation: Having a sponsor and sponsoring others keeps me growing.

Reflection: Am I willing to talk to my sponsor about all the issues that affect my recovery? Do I give the people I sponsor adequate time and attention?

Let Us Write and Reflect
on the Past Week

∽ܐ∾

Did I attend an adequate number of meetings?

Did I exercise too little or too much?

Did I take a Tenth Step inventory on a daily basis?

Was I accountable and honest about my food planning and implementation?

What steps did I practice?

Was I resentful, angry, selfish, dishonest or fearful?

Was I generous, kind, tolerant, patient or useful?

Were my actions, words or communications unloving or unkind?

Do I need to ask for or grant forgiveness for my actions or attitudes this week?

Was my level of hydration adequate?

Did I practice sound nutrition, including vitamins and high-quality foods?

Have I kept something to myself that should be discussed with my sponsor, advisor or therapist?

What areas of my life need improvement?

What service did I perform to help another or my group?

What was my major character flaw this week?

What was my most admirable trait this week?

Did I practice restraint of tongue and pen?

Did I rationalize any destructive behavior?

What are the corrective actions that need to be taken based on this week's inventory? Do I owe any amends?

Diets Don't Work

A diet won't work for a food addict because we have a progressive, chronic, terminal disease. Treating addiction with a diet would be like putting a Band-Aid on a fatal wound. It isn't enough.

When we focus on weight loss instead of recovery, it is exactly like going on a diet. Our motives are not appropriate for the condition. Eventually we come to recognize that when we focus on weight, we lose recovery; when we focus on recovery, we lose weight.

A weight-loss thought might go something like this: *I guess I need to lose weight, I will go on a diet. Guess I'll buy a magazine and look for a good one.* A recovery thought, inspired by a Twelve Step program, might be more like this: *I am a food addict and cannot manage my own life; no human power can relieve my food addiction; I will seek the help of God and the support of other recovering food addicts.*

∽o∾

Affirmation: *I have power from the Highest Source.*

Reflection: *Have I sought a spiritual solution for my addictive disease of powerlessness? Do I seek this solution every day?*

You First? Me First? Recovery First!

In food recovery programs, we often meet people who put everyone else first. People pleasing is a tremendous barrier to our recovery, because recovery must be prioritized.

Because we come into recovery feeling pretty badly about ourselves, our self-esteem is at an all-time low. We've been embarrassed by our appearance and our behavior. We see ourselves as failures. This sense of failure persists in the early years of recovery. We try to make it up to those around us. Rather than making genuine amends, we people please. After all, haven't we had enough trouble in our lives? Motivated by guilt and fear, we placate and appease others, work hard at pleasing those around us, take on everybody's responsibilities and get lost in the process.

The problem with people pleasing is that our needs don't get met. We are motivated by fear of rejection, loss of approval and loneliness. Our recovery process can get lost in this fear and guilt. However, if we stick with it, grow in the program and remain abstinent, we can find the positive potential in the people-pleasing behavior. We can learn to make amends and be useful to others in a healthy way.

∽〇∾

Affirmation: I am worthy of lasting recovery based on love and service.

Reflection: How can I learn to act generously out of love instead of fear and guilt?

Hugs, Not Drugs

Each of us has his or her own
natural pharmacopoeia—the very finest
drugstore available at the cheapest cost—to produce
all the drugs we ever need to run our body/mind
in precisely the way it was designed to
run over centuries of evolution.

Candace Pert, *Molecules of Emotion*

Let's choose wellness, health and joy! Each healthy choice we make reinforces recovery and helps bring our body/mind into balance.

The Twelve Step program includes the healthy principles of abstinence, prayer, meditation, fellowship, surrender, honesty, character building, amends, forgiveness, love and service. We can add other healthy choices that reinforce recovery such as hydration, breath work, outdoor activity, exercise, bodywork, vitamins, humor, play and stress reduction tools, to name a few. In recovery, we feel better the natural way.

For good feelings, using our inner resources beats the artificial use of addictive substances every time.

❧

Affirmation: *I walk outdoors breathing deeply.*

Reflection: *Am I willing to take the time to add exercise, nature and outside air to my healthy choices?*

Bodylove

God made us in his image. He gave us free will to choose the path we want to follow. He made each of us differently: different shapes, sizes, intellects, wants and needs. He gives us remarkable gifts and talents, with the power to develop them through his love and grace.

Our bodies are God's temple here on Earth. We get closer to God when we become willing to treat our bodies with the acceptance, love and gentleness that He intended.

Our security, our sense of self-worth, and our usefulness to God and to our fellows comes not from how we look to the world, but from where our hearts are in relation to God.

࿎

Affirmation: I show gratitude by caring for the body God gave me.

Reflection: Do I love and appreciate my body?

Living in the Moment

*It is not the experience of today that
drives people mad—it is the remorse or bitterness
for something which happened yesterday and
the dread of what tomorrow may bring.*

Unknown author

Two days—yesterday and tomorrow—have no joy. That is why we practice living in the moment.

The here and now gives us a clean slate where we can start fresh every day, every moment. Instead of getting bogged down in the old ways and means of doing things, we can start anew with fresh ideas and enthusiasm. Growth and change take place in the present moment. The power is here, and what we do with it will create the pattern of our lives.

We meet our Higher Power in the present. The only way for us to practice the presence of God is to be fully conscious in the moment. Living in the present we are able to keep finding the God of our understanding, to invite the Power into our lives, and to raise our consciousness of God's gifts of peace and serenity.

࿇

Affirmation: I live fully in the moment with the God of my understanding.

Reflection: Am I willing to consciously let go of the remorse of the past and the dread of the future? Am I willing to invite God into my life right now?

Attainable Affirmations:
A Fabulous Food Plan

Like Goldilocks in the bears' house, we were always eating too little or too much. Now it's great, our food plan is just right! As St. Augustine is credited with saying, "Complete abstinence is easier than perfect moderation."

∽◦∾

I am unconditionally abstinent.
I accept and appreciate my food plan without alteration
or reservation. It is just right for me.

Let Us Write and Reflect
on the Past Week

～○～

Did I attend an adequate number of meetings?

Did I exercise too little or too much?

Did I take a Tenth Step inventory on a daily basis?

Was I accountable and honest about my food planning and implementation?

What steps did I practice?

Was I resentful, angry, selfish, dishonest or fearful?

Was I generous, kind, tolerant, patient or useful?

Were my actions, words or communications unloving or unkind?

Do I need to ask for or grant forgiveness for my actions or attitudes this week?

Was my level of hydration adequate?

Did I practice sound nutrition, including vitamins and high-quality foods?

Have I kept something to myself that should be discussed with my sponsor, advisor or therapist?

What areas of my life need improvement?

What service did I perform to help another or my group?

What was my major character flaw this week?

What was my most admirable trait this week?

Did I practice restraint of tongue and pen?

Did I rationalize any destructive behavior?

What are the corrective actions that need to be taken based on this week's inventory? Do I owe any amends?

Trust God

Recently a friend wrote: "I know God must have another plan for me. I just don't like being kept in the dark." I had recently been thinking about this very concept. When everything works out and we look back, we can see the lesson, but when we are *in* it, our self-will surfaces and we are sure that we know best.

This past week, some life issues have worked out according to the exquisite will of God. When I was in the lesson, I kept getting the spiritual reminder: Trust God, trust God, trust God. I did from time to time, but not consistently. One day I even blew my stack in anger and frustration. But now that more has been revealed, I can only say, "Wow, God *can* do for us what we cannot do for ourselves." In fact, when I look back at this situation, I tried to do exactly what God did accomplish, and I had nothing to do with the final outcome. God did it entirely on His own.

So now I see, once again: Things are not always what they seem. More will be revealed. God's will, not mine, be done! We know that after one door closes, another always opens. Waiting in the hallway, however, is tough.

෴

Affirmation: *I let go and let God.*

Reflection: *What are the consequences of attempting to control outcomes? What are the benefits of waiting for God's plans to be revealed?*

Inventory

Avoiding Step Four is a relapse trap! The only thing this step requires is a legal pad, pen, the AA Big Book and the willingness to examine our past.

First, we study the first 164 pages of this book carefully. Then we take out pen and paper and prayerfully begin writing according to the directions on pages 63 through 71. We keep our written work in a secure place. After listing our resentments, faults, fears, sex conduct and harms done, we evaluate by reviewing our lists, determining their meaning and identifying the lessons learned from our inventory.

Only one Fourth Step is necessary. Step Ten provides for spot checks, and daily and annual reviews.

∽∘∾

Affirmation: *Inventory keeps my side of the street clean.*

Reflection: *Have I completed a thorough Fourth Step? Do I keep my inventory work current by daily and annual inventories?*

Dwell on What You Want

What you think upon grows.

Philippians 4:8

Pray it: Align your mind with God's mind.
Say it: Affirming words are powerful.
See it: Visualize it.
Be it: You have it.

∽o∽

Affirmation: *I affirm the good in life. I dwell on what I want so that I get more of it.*

Reflection: *Am I willing to pray, affirm, visualize and experience the outcome of my dreams? Do I dwell on negative or positive things?*

It Takes a Lie to Start a Binge

Can we really be honest and eat addictively? Honest eating would be something like this: "The last time I ate binge food, I waited until everyone had gone to bed. I snuck around opening packages so that no one could hear the wrapper sounds. I couldn't stop. I ate until I was sick to my stomach. I ate everything in the house, then went out to the convenience store in my nightwear to get more. The next day, I woke up with a hangover and missed work. I was fired from my job. Being unable to pay my bills, I binged over all my troubles. I got sicker and had a gallbladder attack. My health insurance had been canceled so I had to recover without medical assistance."

Do I hear myself saying: "Give me a bowl of that sticky, greasy, pasty stuff, because I sure do want to repeat *that* experience"? After we find our truth in Step One, it always takes a lie to eat binge food again. It takes a lie to start a binge! The lies go like this: "I can handle it. Just one won't hurt. I will get back on food plan tomorrow. No one will know the difference. I don't care."

This is the path of denial, our way of blocking awareness of those destructive eating patterns and the horrible consequences.

༺༠༻

Affirmation: *The truth does set me free. I eat safe food in a safe way.*

Reflection: *Am I willing to write the honest tale of my last binge as a reminder that it takes a lie to start a binge?*

The Nontoxic Shopping Experience

How about practicing tolerant, compassionate love in the marketplace? Let's meditate on the idea that we will stop complaining to management about an employee no matter what he or she has done. Instead we can say, "Bless them, change me," and understand that our complaints might spread pain far and wide.

Anyone can have a bad moment, experience a lapse of judgment or feel irritable. We can allow them that momentary failure while we remember that love is the only principle that we need to practice. That employee deserves love—no matter what.

When we bring love to a situation rather than animosity, we are controlling our response, staying in a place of love and experiencing peace and happiness.

∽○∽

Affirmation: *Bless them, change me.*

Reflection: *Am I willing to act—not react—to another's bad moments? Will I learn acceptance in the marketplace by sparing someone the pain of my animosity?*

Recognition, Admission, Acceptance

We can deny the truth, but we can't change it.

Once a food addict, always a food addict. There are so many ways to avoid that truth. We can rationalize, justify, avoid and evade, but the truth remains the same: We have lost control over food.

We take the First Step in order to change. We recognize our powerlessness, admit and accept it at gut level. Try as we might, willpower was never enough. So we reach out for a Higher Power to restore our lives through unconditional abstinence, emotional maturation and spiritual practices. We find support and direction in our recovery groups where we learn that we cannot change people, places and things either. So we change within and leave the outer environment in God's hands.

∽∾

Affirmation: I focus on changing me.

Reflection: Do I recognize, admit and accept that I cannot change or control my outer environment? Am I willing to work on myself?

Let Us Write and Reflect
on the Past Week

∽o∽

Did I attend an adequate number of meetings?

Did I exercise too little or too much?

Did I take a Tenth Step inventory on a daily basis?

Was I accountable and honest about my food planning and implementation?

What steps did I practice?

Was I resentful, angry, selfish, dishonest or fearful?

Was I generous, kind, tolerant, patient or useful?

Were my actions, words or communications unloving or unkind?

Do I need to ask for or grant forgiveness for my actions or attitudes this week?

Was my level of hydration adequate?

Did I practice sound nutrition, including vitamins and high-quality foods?

Have I kept something to myself that should be discussed with my sponsor, advisor or therapist?

What areas of my life need improvement?

What service did I perform to help another or my group?

What was my major character flaw this week?

What was my most admirable trait this week?

Did I practice restraint of tongue and pen?

Did I rationalize any destructive behavior?

What are the corrective actions that need to be taken based on this week's inventory? Do I owe any amends?

Today's Stress Buster:
Honesty

Dishonesty is very stressful. Besides making us anxious and mistrustful, keeping track of lies is debilitating, exhausting and a major source of human distress.

The three forms of dishonesty are lies we tell others, lies we tell ourselves and lies of omission (when we say nothing). Living an ethical existence is stabilizing and centering. Honest people enjoy healthy powerful lives. They are open and authentic, sharing their thoughts, feelings, pasts and plans with others.

Honesty is the *healthy* policy.

The Twelve Steps are the spiritual principles that guide us in our personal recovery. The founders of AA came up with twelve principles—Traditions—that keep our groups intact. These Twelve Traditions are to the groups what the Twelve Steps are to the individual. They are suggested principles that ensure the survival and growth of the group. Hammered out on the anvil of experience, they were designed to guide our groups. Personal survival and survival of our program depend on understanding and implementing these principles. We need to develop a personal regard for the Twelve Traditions and an awareness of our role in preserving the unity of our Twelve Step program. In recovery, we become practitioners of the Twelve Steps *and* the Twelve Traditions.

TRADITION FOUR

"Each group should be autonomous except in matters affecting other groups or [the fellowship] as a whole."

Our groups can do as they wish, as long as they do not impact negatively upon surrounding groups or the fellowship as a whole. Every group has autonomy in its own affairs. They can make any decisions they like. No authority may challenge their right to do so. A group can even violate the traditions without interference if they so desire.

The line is drawn when the group's decisions affect neighboring groups and the fellowship as a whole. If a group wishes to take any action that will affect others, surrounding groups, intergroup and/or World Services should be consulted.

On a personal level, we make it clear that we are not representatives of our Twelve Step program; we consider the welfare of all our groups and the rest of the fellowship.

❧

Affirmation: I safeguard the welfare of the fellowship.
Reflection: Do I take a larger view of the decisions of my group by evaluating how they impact on our fellowship as a whole?

Live and Let Live

For years, our lives as active addicts were built on self-will. People and things were good or bad in relation to how they fit our desires and plans. Even when our intentions were good, we often ended up on a collision course with somebody else. We reacted with anger and harbored resentments, and our tantrums ended in a binge.

In recovery, we learn that emotional binges are deadly too. Now we are learning to "live and let live." That is the path of tolerance, a sign of emotional maturity.

Tolerance is willingness to give up judging others' opinions, beliefs and behaviors. This attitude of "live and let live," which is a way to cope with differences, is essential to our comfort. Tolerance disagrees agreeably. That's why in recovery, we agree to disagree. We come to see that others have the right to live as they see fit, just as we expect to live as we choose.

∽○∾

Affirmation: *I humbly ask God to remove my intolerance.*

Reflection: *Do I humbly accept my fellows just the way they are today? What can I do differently to become more tolerant?*

Freely Given

"Service asks for nothing, not even respect." When my sponsor spoke those words, it really made me think. We do service without expectation of reward of any kind. In early recovery, our sponsors usually introduce us to service work—opening meetings, taking care of literature, setting up and cleaning up the meeting room, and making phone calls. Service work is doing what is needed to keep our meetings going. Later we discover other levels of service such as leading meetings, sponsoring, serving at regional and world levels.

So why do we do it? Service gets us out of ourselves, blesses us and others, and keeps us from picking up that first bite. In service, we demonstrate that we are responsible and reliable, which raises our level of self-esteem. Service work keeps our program thriving and available for the new person.

❦

Affirmation: I help carry the message by giving service.

Reflection: Do I offer to open meetings and clean up afterward?

Unconditionally Abstinent

Our disease is rigid and unforgiving. The tiniest amount of a trigger substance will result in a reaction. A food plan eliminates all triggers for those who are addicted to food.

Some people have suggested that food plans are rigid, but we call them effective. We no longer debate about abstinence; we recover using the best plan we can find.

Now that we know the exact nature of our affliction, we understand that the elimination of trigger foods, volume, compulsive eating and spontaneous eating are crucial for our health and well-being. Departures from the food plan are deadly. They result in creeping relapse.

We might be tempted to think that deviations will bring satisfaction. Maybe more food, different food or different combinations will satisfy us. Such thoughts are false. Deviation results in expanding deviations, never satisfaction. The safe way is to practice the food plan as written—unconditionally.

We deserve clean abstinence, which is the foundation of recovery.

〰

Affirmation: I practice unconditional abstinence.

Reflection: Do I give myself permission to deviate from the food plan? What are the risks of such deviations?

Choices

Our choices do not always seem so clear when we are speeding along in the disease process. Denial, delusion and dishonesty support the idea that we can return to normal eating anytime we wish.

The world is full of easy-appearing choices. Which shall it be: painful surgery or reliance on God? Which shall it be: another diet, therapy, shot, pill or doctor, or asking God for help? Which shall it be: endless bingeing or God's way? Which shall it be: my plan or God's plan?

We are told that God can do for us what we cannot do for ourselves. We see Him working in others' lives. However, a monumental mental and spiritual conversion is needed to break the idea that we can eat like other people.

We came to accept the fact that our eating is out of control and that our lives are not working. Without help, we cannot stop. Through the continuing daily surrender of our will to God's will, we come to experience less turmoil, more peace with food.

∽∘∾

Affirmation: *I choose God's will for me today.*

Reflection: *How do I determine when my will is getting in the way?*

Let Us Write and Reflect
on the Past Week

〜〜

Did I attend an adequate number of meetings?

Did I exercise too little or too much?

Did I take a Tenth Step inventory on a daily basis?

Was I accountable and honest about my food planning and implementation?

What steps did I practice?

Was I resentful, angry, selfish, dishonest or fearful?

Was I generous, kind, tolerant, patient or useful?

Were my actions, words or communications unloving or unkind?

Do I need to ask for or grant forgiveness for my actions or attitudes this week?

Was my level of hydration adequate?

Did I practice sound nutrition, including vitamins and high-quality foods?

Have I kept something to myself that should be discussed with my sponsor, advisor or therapist?

What areas of my life need improvement?

What service did I perform to help another or my group?

What was my major character flaw this week?

What was my most admirable trait this week?

Did I practice restraint of tongue and pen?

Did I rationalize any destructive behavior?

What are the corrective actions that need to be taken based on this week's inventory? Do I owe any amends?

Please, Eat It for Me

One of our friends shares her experience: "One of my relapse warning signs is 'vicarious eating.' I would innocently buy non-abstinent treats for the nonaddicts in my life and then get a kick out of watching them eat it for me. This game came back to haunt me when I got obsessed with one particular food and ended up eating it myself four days later. I got hold of that obsession and would not let it go. It led me to full-blown relapse."

A psychological truth is that we move toward our dominant thought. When we are obsessed with the kinds of food that will trigger our disease, we are moving toward eating that food.

The mind is a powerful instrument. In recovery, we take charge of our thoughts and become the masters of our minds. Our "old ideas" about food must be challenged and examined.

One of the characteristics of food addiction is obsession with food. When we stay in the obsession, we stay in the disease. A way to deal with self-defeating thoughts of food is to identify, challenge and change them.

We see food differently now! The addictive foods we obsess about are poison for us and may be for our loved ones too.

∽o∾

Affirmation: I focus on nutritious food. It is the most attractive choice.

Reflection: How will I challenge old ideas and replace them with recovery thoughts?

Let Us Write and Reflect on
the Following Question

⤕⤔

What are three things I would like to change about myself? Why?

_____

_____

_____

_____

_____

_____

_____

_____

_____

_____

_____

_____

_____

_____

_____

Ignoring the Facts Does Not Change the Facts

A rose by any other name smells just as sweet, and a perfumed skunk is still a skunk.

Looking at food addiction as "just a weight-loss issue" does not change the fact of addiction. We received a message about the food plan from a woman who said, "The only way I would attempt a diet like that would be if I was terminal and the diet would prolong my life or something." Guess what? She *is* terminal!

Food addiction is chronic, progressive and fatal. The food plan would prolong her life. Blocking the awareness of the truth does not change the facts. Denial of any aspect of the disease process impairs progress by locking us into destructive patterns.

Every one of the Twelve Steps helps us break patterns. By their use we identify and eliminate attitudes, beliefs and behaviors that keep us from experiencing glorious recovery.

ھﻮﻮ

Affirmation: I am breaking patterns by doing the next right thing.

Reflection: Am I willing to identify one stuck place that keeps me from going forward in recovery?

Nothing Tastes as Good as Abstinence Feels

Abstinent food is better, abstinent life is better, abstinent thinking and behavior are better, so why would we even consider ditching abstinence for a bite of addictive food?

A friend shares, "When I have broken my abstinence in the past, it has been because I have forgotten for just a moment the pain of eating that first bite." We do have efficient forgetters! They seem to be built into food addicts. We can forget both the pain of the disease and the joy of recovery in just a moment unless we stay close to other program members who share the consequences of the illness and the benefits of recovery.

At meetings we recall "what it was like, what happened and what it is like now."

∽୦∾

Affirmation: I practice unconditional abstinence from all addictive triggers.

Reflection: Do I remember the consequences of food addiction? What are the benefits of recovery?

Let Us Write and Reflect
on the Following Idea

Can you imagine how different your life would be if you could say with absolute surety, "I am in charge of my money. Yes, I am. No doubt about it"?

Ruth Hayden

The World Is My Abstinent Place

We have a portable program. It goes everywhere with us—around the block or to Europe—and because of that, the world is our abstinent place.

When abstinent eating, thinking and living becomes a commitment, then the dominant thought becomes, *How do I maintain recovery right here, right now—this place, this time?* A practical answer to that question is always available.

Sometimes we have to think creatively in order to fill our recovery needs as we move through the world. For instance, a friend in London called together an impromptu meeting in an Internet chat room because there were no convenient meetings in her immediate geographic area. Using our telephones, computers and literature, we can create our own "meetings between meetings."

Food can be managed while traveling by being assertive in restaurants. Order all food to be served plain: protein with no marinade, baked potato and steamed veggies or salad. Carry an over-the-shoulder soft cooler and dressings in little containers. Freeze one cup of measured cooked grains in plastic bags. Take cans of tuna and beans and frozen vegetable loaves for plane rides. Request an in-room refrigerator at the hotel. Don't forget to take literature. Ask your sponsor for a written assignment for downtime when you are on the road!

∞∞

Affirmation: I take my program with me wherever I go: down the road, across the continent and over the ocean.

Reflection: Am I willing to go to any lengths to stay abstinent during my travels, or do I see my trip as a vacation from recovery disciplines?

Let Us Write and Reflect
on the Past Week

∽o∾

Did I attend an adequate number of meetings?

Did I exercise too little or too much?

Did I take a Tenth Step inventory on a daily basis?

Was I accountable and honest about my food planning and implementation?

What steps did I practice?

Was I resentful, angry, selfish, dishonest or fearful?

Was I generous, kind, tolerant, patient or useful?

Were my actions, words or communications unloving or unkind?

Do I need to ask for or grant forgiveness for my actions or attitudes this week?

Was my level of hydration adequate?

Did I practice sound nutrition, including vitamins and high-quality foods?

Have I kept something to myself that should be discussed with my sponsor, advisor or therapist?

What areas of my life need improvement?

What service did I perform to help another or my group?

What was my major character flaw this week?

What was my most admirable trait this week?

Did I practice restraint of tongue and pen?

Did I rationalize any destructive behavior?

What are the corrective actions that need to be taken based on this week's inventory? Do I owe any amends?

If You Do What You Always Did, You'll Get What You Always Got

Isn't it amazing that the same behavior always brings the same result? That is a scientific concept. If a scientist kept on repeating the same experiment while expecting different results, we would question such methods. When the scientific method is applied, and the experiments bear out the hypothesis (the assumption that is being tested), the connection may come to be regarded as a theory or law of nature. An experiment that does not bear out the hypothesis is rejected or modified.

So in life, especially the life of a food addict, we act upon certain assumptions or hypotheses. "This time I will eat just one." Usually this assumption is followed by the ingestion of more than one—many more!

Is the hypothesis rejected by the food addict? The experiment goes on for years, decades even. Every time the food addict's experiment fails to support the hypothesis that he or she can eat just one, the data is discarded in favor of another experiment. *Let's just try this again. This time I will do better! I can get this right. I know I have self-control—I will stop!*

Addicts do the same thing over and over expecting different results. We experience the same lesson repeatedly *until we learn the lesson!* "Hey, I finally figured it out. I can't eat just one."

The same holds true throughout the course of recovery. We continue to test and validate or discard our assumptions. We learn to become vigilant and aware; we have guidance from others in recovery; we follow the path of the Twelve Steps. In this process, we start to identify our patterns and change our assumptions. We gain insight. We make better choices. We learn how to stop the pain.

∽∘∽

Affirmation: I learn and grow because I make valid choices.
Reflection: Do I base my life on lessons learned or false hypotheses?

"Whisper Words of Wisdom: Let It Be"

What a peaceful word "let" is. We can float on the softness of it. It is an ego-buster! Let go! Let God! Let it be!

As the song says, "There will be an answer: Let it be." That is so contrary to our nature as "fixers." We just want to get in there and fix everything, yet how often the answer is to let it be, let it go.

The top ten categories of things to let go of are:

- What other people think, say and do
- Blaming
- The past and future
- Expectations
- Old ideas
- Getting my way
- Relationships
- Being right
- Judgments
- Resentments

∽∘∾

Affirmation: *When I am uptight, I whisper "let it be."*

Reflection: *How will I let go of the old in order to make room for the new?*

Mother Nature

The people of the Six Nations, also known as Iroquois Confederacy, call themselves the *Hau de no sau nee,* the People of the Longhouse. Located in the northeastern region of North America, the Six Nations included the Mohawks, Oneidas, Onondagas, Cayugas, Seneca and the Tuscaroras.

My friend Alva is a native who lives on the Six Nations Reserve in Ontario, Canada. Since my great-grandmother was born into the Canadian Mohawk nation of the Six Nations Confederacy, I often have questions for Alva. Recently I asked her, "What would our great-grandmothers have thought about those little three-dollar bottles of drinking water we buy?" Alva answered in her serene voice, "If you don't take care of Mother Nature, you will pay!"

We must face this fact. Whenever we break Mother Nature's laws, we pay on many levels: personally, environmentally, morally, financially.

According to the Hau de no sau nee:

> *The original instructions direct that we who walk about on the Earth are to express a great respect, an affection, and a gratitude toward all the spirits which create and support Life . . . the grain, beans, squash, the winds, the sun. When people cease to respect and express gratitude for these many things, then all life will be destroyed, and human life on this planet will come to an end.*

∽∘∾

Affirmation: *I thank my Creator for the things of the Earth that support my life. I give thanks by taking care of Mother Nature.*

Reflection: *Am I willing to recycle, waste nothing and play an active role in environmental issues?*

God Speaking

All which I took from thee I did but take,
not for thy harms, but just that thou might'st seek it in
My arms. All which thy child's mistake fancies
as lost, I have stored for thee at home:
Rise, clasp My hand, and come.

Francis Thompson, *The Hound of Heaven*

The words above remind me that any loss that sends me closer to God is really a gain. The poet, who suffered from opium addiction, writes about hitting bottom and finding God, whom he had eluded for so many years.

His poem is the story of our addiction too. When considering our losses in addiction, we realize that our losses made room for our greater gifts in recovery. These gifts are found when we grasp our Higher Power's hand and walk out of the darkness into the light.

∽∽∽

Affirmation: *I walk in the light of the spirit.*

Reflection: *What separates me from God? What keeps me close?*

Help

I love that "Help" word on my computer tool bar. Every time I wonder how to do something on my computer, I can click on "help," and instructions pop up, plain and simple. There it is right in front of me. Help—a very important word.

The whole idea of recovery is about learning to ask for help, and what a terrifying thing that can be. Our whole ego structure cries out against it.

Asking for face-to-face help isn't quite as simple as clicking the mouse. It takes a lot of humility, but practice makes it easier and the payoff is spectacular. Upon asking, we can receive support, encouragement, problem-solving techniques, spiritual guidance and prayers for successful outcomes. All we have to do is get past the queasy feeling before we ask, find the right person and then follow directions.

Ask and you shall receive.

∽◦∾

Affirmation: *Wherever I go, there are people willing to help me.*

Reflection: *What is the outcome when I resist asking for help? What happens when I am willing to ask for help?*

Need a Meeting?

A friend who gained weight in relapse wanted to lose the weight before going back to meetings. She said, "Isn't it funny that when we need it the most, we don't want to go to meetings because someone might notice (gasp) that we're food addicts? That's like having pneumonia, but not wanting to go to the doctor until we are better. It surely does show that we are insane, doesn't it?"

People who don't go to meetings don't hear about what happens to people who don't go to meetings. Just about everything we learn about recovery and relapse is at meetings.

No excuse ever kept us from getting to our binge food. No excuse can keep us from meetings when we want recovery.

∽∞∾

Affirmation: *My meeting is the place to share and heal.*

Reflection: *What do recovery meetings mean to me?*

Let Us Write and Reflect
on the Past Week

༺○༻

Did I attend an adequate number of meetings?

Did I exercise too little or too much?

Did I take a Tenth Step inventory on a daily basis?

Was I accountable and honest about my food planning and implementation?

What steps did I practice?

Was I resentful, angry, selfish, dishonest or fearful?

Was I generous, kind, tolerant, patient or useful?

Were my actions, words or communications unloving or unkind?

Do I need to ask for or grant forgiveness for my actions or attitudes this week?

Was my level of hydration adequate?

Did I practice sound nutrition, including vitamins and high-quality foods?

Have I kept something to myself that should be discussed with my sponsor, advisor or therapist?

What areas of my life need improvement?

What service did I perform to help another or my group?

What was my major character flaw this week?

What was my most admirable trait this week?

Did I practice restraint of tongue and pen?

Did I rationalize any destructive behavior?

What are the corrective actions that need to be taken based on this week's inventory? Do I owe any amends?

Attainable Affirmations:
Go in Peace

Negativity is tiring. Whether we want to be negative or not is our decision. We can always choose to practice the principles embodied in the Twelve Steps. In that way, we can work our way out of negativity.

∽०∾

I live in peace and harmony with all living things.

May Day

May Day is a celebration of happiness, joy and the coming of summer. It signals the end of a hard winter and the beginning of sunshine and flowers.

Instead of dancing around the Maypole, let's play a spirited dance collection and dance around the house. That is a fun exercise experience! If you are alone for this exercise, you will be laughing out loud. If others are around, I guarantee that everyone will be laughing.

∽○∽

Affirmation: *I freely express my joy and laughter.*

Reflection: *Wouldn't it be fun to have a sock hop in the living room?*

Recognizing Relapse

In order to recover, we must recognize relapse. A friend says, "Relapse happens when I start stopping things—such as daily inventory, meetings, phone calls!"

She is right on! Relapse is imminent when we stop using the tools of recovery. Daily inventory reveals troublesome patterns emerging in our recovery programs. Evaluating and correcting trouble spots before they go out of control keeps us on the path of strong recovery.

∽o∽

Affirmation: *My recovery program is current.*

Reflection: *Do I meet minimum daily program requirements for recovery? What are those requirements?*

Promises of Step Five

*We admitted to God, to ourselves and to another
human being the exact nature of our wrongs.*

*Once we have taken this step, withholding nothing, we
are delighted. We can look the world in the eye. We can be
alone at perfect peace and ease. Our fears fall from us. We
begin to feel the nearness of our Creator. We may have had
certain spiritual beliefs, but now we begin to have a spiritual
experience. The feeling that the drink [food] problem has disappeared will often come strongly. We feel we are on the
Broad Highway, walking hand in hand with the Spirit of the
Universe.*

Alcoholics Anonymous, p. 75

Today's Stress Buster:
Play

When I was a kid, whenever I went out the door during nonschool times, I went out to play. Addiction ended playtime for many of us. Let's find it again.

How about walking in the rain, splashing in puddles, smelling flowers, blowing bubbles, playing real-time Internet games, building sand castles, watching the sun rise or set, greeting everyone you meet with a word and a smile, kicking off your shoes, planning an adventure, singing in the shower, playing with a pet, wearing a spoon on your nose, kicking a can, making a campfire for friends and neighbors, dancing, flying kites, skipping, whirling, twirling or laughing, all for the fun of it?

Play is a great self-help technique, getting us into the here and now, reducing stress, energizing and generating spontaneity and creativity. Besides all that, it releases negative energy and places us in a healthy relationship with others by promoting communication and empathy.

Bingo anyone? Plan some playtime and enjoy being a kid again.

꿍

Affirmation: *I enjoy healthy fun and play.*

Reflection: *Have I scheduled playtime this week?*

Accountability

Daily, in terms of our conduct and reactions, we make choices that contribute to our personal improvement or decline. We are accountable for our lives: our process and our progress. "The buck stops here!"

As tempted as we are to blame people, places and events for our troubles, the bottom line is that we are responsible for our own health and happiness. The law of cause and effect comes into play. If we overeat, drink to excess or disregard good sleep habits, we will pay the price of deteriorating physical health. When we criticize and live with resentment, fear and expectations, we will suffer spiritual and emotional pain.

Our physical, emotional and spiritual well-being is under our control. We are not victims. We are powerful beings, the product of our own choices.

∾◦∾

Affirmation: *I create excellent health by practicing healthy behaviors and reactions.*

Reflection: *Am I willing to accept the consequences of my choices? What are three better choices I could make today?*

Let Us Write and Reflect
on the Past Week

❧

Did I attend an adequate number of meetings?

Did I exercise too little or too much?

Did I take a Tenth Step inventory on a daily basis?

Was I accountable and honest about my food planning and implementation?

What steps did I practice?

Was I resentful, angry, selfish, dishonest or fearful?

Was I generous, kind, tolerant, patient or useful?

Were my actions, words or communications unloving or unkind?

Do I need to ask for or grant forgiveness for my actions or attitudes this week?

Was my level of hydration adequate?

Did I practice sound nutrition, including vitamins and high-quality foods?

Have I kept something to myself that should be discussed with my sponsor, advisor or therapist?

What areas of my life need improvement?

What service did I perform to help another or my group?

What was my major character flaw this week?

What was my most admirable trait this week?

Did I practice restraint of tongue and pen?

Did I rationalize any destructive behavior?

What are the corrective actions that need to be taken based on this week's inventory? Do I owe any amends?

Off Again, On Again

Can we go off the food plan and get right back on? This type of thinking is dangerous. It does not take into account the idea of powerlessness.

We may be able to get abstinent again after eating addictive food. However, take into consideration these facts: When eating addictive foods, all progress in recovery stops, we go back to zero. We may be able to recapture our abstinence, we may not. Many who relapse do not. We all have another binge left in us, but do we have another recovery?

Picking up addictive foods may condemn us to spending the rest of our life struggling in active disease. We cannot predict what will happen when we pick up. We get into recovery to have a better life. To continue to go through the discomfort of experiencing active disease and withdrawals is too painful to contemplate. Getting abstinent and staying abstinent in order to build a successful life is so much easier.

Stabilizing takes time. Why continuously disrupt that stabilization process by returning to active addiction? I like a friend's approach. I have heard her say many times, "I do not intend to get abstinent again." With devoted attention to recovery, we don't have to!

∽o∾

Affirmation: *I willingly and gratefully maintain abstinence.*

Reflection: *How do I give myself permission to go off food plan? Am I willing to correct these deviations from the plan?*

Exercise

Every healthy choice supports recovery. Exercise is one of those healthy choices that brings our body and brain chemistry into balance. It is a look-good, feel-good, be-good choice.

Why not consider walking for a regular exercise program? It will improve stamina, energy levels and quality of life. Walking can help reduce health risks such as arthritis, coronary heart disease, osteoporosis and anxiety. A good walk is a stress reducer. Then there are the social aspects of walking when we include friends and neighbors.

Walking works anywhere, at any time. All it takes is a good pair of shoes and the willingness to walk out the door or hop on a treadmill. A special pleasure is walking in the natural world—on the beach or through a park—to enjoy the open air and the feel-good peptides produced by enhanced movement and breathing.

∽○∽

Affirmation: *I appreciate the good feelings of movement.*

Reflection: *Do I exercise on a regular basis? What excuses keep me from enjoying exercise?*

Dealing with Stress

If a group of people in recovery listed the problems they face and then looked at the common factors on their lists, one commonality would be that everyone experiences stress.

Despite the fact that everyone experiences stress, some people are happy and others are unhappy. What is the difference between happy and unhappy people? The answer involves something other than stress, because everyone experiences it on a daily basis. One difference between these groups is that the coping strategy of happy people works. Unhappy people don't cope effectively. A coping strategy is a combination of our thoughts, feelings and behaviors. When we experience a stressful disturbance, we tell ourselves something, we feel something and then we do something.

In the past, most of us "ate over the stress." People who stay in recovery have to find a better way to deal with the disturbance and the feelings that surface.

The Twelve Steps and every tool of recovery provide ways of dealing with stress. People who are happy in recovery use the tools of meetings, phone calls, literature, prayer and meditation as means of coping with stress.

∽◦∽

Affirmation: *I manage stress by using the right recovery tool.*

Reflection: *How does my recovery program help me through stressful times? Which tools do I depend on when times are tough?*

The Twelve Steps are the spiritual principles that guide us in our personal recovery. The founders of AA came up with twelve principles—Traditions—that keep our groups intact. These Twelve Traditions are to the groups what the Twelve Steps are to the individual. They are suggested principles that ensure the survival and growth of the group. Hammered out on the anvil of experience, they were designed to guide our groups. Personal survival and survival of our program depend on understanding and implementing these principles. We need to develop a personal regard for the Twelve Traditions and an awareness of our role in preserving the unity of our Twelve Step program. In recovery, we become practitioners of the Twelve Steps *and* the Twelve Traditions.

TRADITION FIVE

*"Each group has but one primary purpose—to carry
its message to the food addict who still suffers."*

We cannot be all things to all people. In our programs, we do one thing well: We carry the message of recovery to the still-suffering food addict. We carry a lifesaving message of hope to those who will surely die from addictive disease—that is our major purpose!

On a personal level, we understand that this tradition applies to us. We stay in touch with newcomers, longtimers (who may be suffering too) and those who have disappeared from our meeting rooms. We remember in our interactions with other members that our primary purpose is to carry the message of recovery. We help our groups fulfill our purpose by making phone calls, taking an active part in meeting preparation, sharing at meetings and Twelve Stepping the newcomer. When visiting other programs, such as AA, we recall this tradition and respect their primary purpose.

∽o∽

Affirmation: *I joyfully share the message of recovery.*
Reflection: *Have I shown responsibility to my group by setting up for meetings, sharing at meetings and calling members who are absent?*

Handling Our Feelings

Addictive substances numb our feelings. We do not learn to handle our feelings in an effective way during the course of our addiction because we "eat over them." Since that option is not available to us in recovery, we learn to deal with our feelings instead.

A good way to get a good handle on our feelings is to realize that we think ourselves into trauma. Our perception of what goes on around us causes our upset. We can challenge and change the thought that creates our toxic feelings.

Change the thought and the feeling will follow.

∽∘∾

Affirmation: *As I change my thoughts, my feelings change.*

Reflection: *Do I ask for help when I am experiencing painful feelings? Am I willing to identify my feelings and the thoughts that create them, then challenge those thoughts and change them?*

The Touchstones of Growth

*When we can see the inevitability of growth
and change, we begin to become motivated
by our dreams, not our deficiencies.*

Greg Anderson

When we do our early inventories, we make a list of character defects—usually topped by our most glaring ones! As we become aware of these defects and willingly perform our spiritual and emotional work, emphasis on our shortcomings begins to take a back seat to a forward plan of positive emotional and spiritual growth.

The ego-puncturing work of early recovery is supplanted by goal setting. "We saw we needn't always be bludgeoned and beaten into humility. It could come quite as much from our voluntary reaching for it as it could from unremitting suffering" (AA, *Twelve Steps and Twelve Traditions*). As we identify the blocks to our growth, we learn to set goals to overcome them.

An annual inventory of all departments of our life is a good start for identifying our aspirations. Once we have listed our objectives, we prioritize them, then develop a plan to achieve them. Next, we make a daily to-do list to break down and clarify the tasks that will help us reach our goals.

༄

Affirmation: *This life in recovery is beyond my wildest dreams!*

Reflection: *Do I have recovery goals? Have I made a list that will reflect the tasks necessary to achieve my recovery growth goals?*

Let Us Write and Reflect
on the Past Week

∽○∾

Did I attend an adequate number of meetings?

Did I exercise too little or too much?

Did I take a Tenth Step inventory on a daily basis?

Was I accountable and honest about my food planning and implementation?

What steps did I practice?

Was I resentful, angry, selfish, dishonest or fearful?

Was I generous, kind, tolerant, patient or useful?

Were my actions, words or communications unloving or unkind?

Do I need to ask for or grant forgiveness for my actions or attitudes this week?

Was my level of hydration adequate?

Did I practice sound nutrition, including vitamins and high-quality foods?

Have I kept something to myself that should be discussed with my sponsor, advisor or therapist?

What areas of my life need improvement?

What service did I perform to help another or my group?

What was my major character flaw this week?

What was my most admirable trait this week?

Did I practice restraint of tongue and pen?

Did I rationalize any destructive behavior?

What are the corrective actions that need to be taken based on this week's inventory? Do I owe any amends?

Self-Respect

Before recovery, we were on a path of self-destruction. The path of addiction is a downward spiral of physical, emotional and spiritual anguish.

Recovery ends the abusive spiral. Recovery provides the opportunity to behave in a way that shows respect for our bodies, minds and spirits. Every act of self-control brings a measure of self-respect. We show regard for our physical bodies by improving nutrition, exercise, sleep and health care. Treating ourselves and others with respect brings us to a greater sense of self-worth.

When we make a good food choice, speak kindly to others or practice patience and generosity, we add to our feelings of self-worth.

∾∾

Affirmation: *I practice respect for myself, respect for others and responsibility for all my actions.*

Reflection: *Do I control my behaviors and my responses in order to show respect for myself and others?*

Silence Is Sometimes the Best Answer

Keeping my mouth shut is really hard. One time an employer said "MYOB." I had no idea what she meant. I asked for a translation, and she said, "Mind your own business." I drew a blank.

I loved to be well-informed about everyone and everything. My "business" was extensive and my comments excessive.

Recovery has narrowed my horizons. I no longer have to comment about everything or answer every question. Listening is good. I have heard that concept in meetings: Learn to listen and listen to learn. This advice is good for someone who had an opinion about everything and interrupted a lot too. Listening is a lesson in communication and humility.

Really good communicators are good listeners. Another thing, the silent answer is a great way to avoid debate. I don't have to argue every point anymore. That comes under the "keeping your mouth shut" heading too. I like the slogan, "We don't debate, we recover."

∽⊶∾

Affirmation: *I leave unnecessary comments unspoken.*

Reflection: *Would I become a better communicator by becoming a better listener?*

Our Character Is Our Destiny

All those people in nursing homes are just what they always were—only more so! The angry get angrier, the sweet get sweeter. What a warning!

What kind of old folks will we be? If we want to improve our destiny, we have to change our character.

The Twelve Steps are the addict's plan for character development. We have learned through our step work that our old way of living is not working. Our motivation is to do better and to be better. We may not think about it as character building, but it is. As we work through the steps, we change and grow—by trusting the God of our understanding, identifying our ineffective character traits through inventory and creating a life of love and service.

❦

Affirmation: *Character building is my conscious choice.*

Reflection: *What is my approach to character building? Today I will review the character-building inventory as described in AA Twelve Steps and Twelve Traditions, p. 88-95.*

Let Us Write and Reflect on
the Following Question

ᔕᦞᔕ

What are my dearest desires, dreams and visions?

_____

_____

_____

_____

_____

_____

_____

_____

_____

_____

_____

_____

_____

_____

_____

_____

_____

Permission Giving

Getting into recovery takes an enormous effort. The changes we make turn our lives around. The various responsibilities of recovery take up our time and attention. Meetings, phone calls, step work and relationships with sponsors and buddies become a way of life. Our program works because we work it!

Somewhere along the way, we give ourselves permission to stop one or another of our recovery tools. Permission giving is a form of rationalizing dangerous behavior. Here are four sets of permission-giving/permission-withdrawing examples:

"I can miss this meeting because the weather is so bad." (How about a phone or online meeting instead?)

"It's okay to skip this meal, I fell asleep." (If you feel sleepy, set the alarm for your meal.)

"I am too busy to make my calls today." (If you are too busy to make calls, you are too busy. Prioritize recovery tasks.)

"I can eat this food; after all it isn't sugar, flour or wheat." (It isn't on the food plan either, so it is an addictive substance.)

∽◦∽

Affirmation: *I give myself permission to strengthen my program today.*

Reflection: *Why not give myself permission to improve my program rather than weaken it? I will initiate one recovery practice today that will enhance my program.*

Not Getting What You Want
Is Sometimes a Blessing

People who are unpracticed in the will of God may fear that God's way may not be trustworthy. One of my friends was afraid that if he "turned his life and will over to God," he might be sent out as a missionary. If that was God's will for him, he didn't want to go.

Like my friend, don't we honestly believe that we are the real experts in our own needs? How could God know better? Since we have spent so much time and attention on ourselves, we must know best. Well, look where that got us!

Learning to trust God's will proves to be a heavenly adventure. Seeing the exquisite and intricate way it works out is astonishing. God always answers our prayer. Sometimes the answer is no, but we trust in the knowledge that the answer is always for our greatest good. So we pray for our greatest good, our greatest healing and the greatest outcome for all involved. God's will be done.

∞o∞

Affirmation: *I pray and welcome what God sends.*

Reflection: *How can I take what God gives me each day and make joy out of it?*

Let Us Write and Reflect
on the Past Week

ﮧﮧﮧ

Did I attend an adequate number of meetings?

Did I exercise too little or too much?

Did I take a Tenth Step inventory on a daily basis?

Was I accountable and honest about my food planning and implementation?

What steps did I practice?

Was I resentful, angry, selfish, dishonest or fearful?

Was I generous, kind, tolerant, patient or useful?

Were my actions, words or communications unloving or unkind?

Do I need to ask for or grant forgiveness for my actions or attitudes this week?

Was my level of hydration adequate?

Did I practice sound nutrition, including vitamins and high-quality foods?

Have I kept something to myself that should be discussed with my sponsor, advisor or therapist?

What areas of my life need improvement?

What service did I perform to help another or my group?

What was my major character flaw this week?

What was my most admirable trait this week?

Did I practice restraint of tongue and pen?

Did I rationalize any destructive behavior?

What are the corrective actions that need to be taken based on this week's inventory? Do I owe any amends?

Let Us Write and Reflect
on the Following Idea

And acceptance is the answer to all *my problems today. When I am disturbed, it is because I find some person, place, thing, or situation—some fact of my life—unacceptable to me, and I can find no serenity until I accept that person, place, thing, or situation as being exactly the way it is supposed to be at this moment.*

Alcoholics Anonymous, p. 449

There Is Only One
Way to Coast—Downhill

Action is the magic word for recovery. Relapse requires no effort. It is spontaneous, occurring in the absence of a strong recovery program.

Coasting is a downhill ride. Recovery is not spontaneous; it requires discipline and commitment. Each stage of recovery—learning, growing, maintaining—requires attention to details.

After we move out of denial, we find out about our addiction and become familiar with the practices of recovery, such as step work, sponsorship and meeting attendance. We grow as we construct a new life based upon changes in our perceptions, values, attitudes and beliefs. Maintenance is built upon continuing inventory, prayer, meditation and service. We live what we have learned and continue to grow. All of the stages of recovery require continuing effort and the daily practice of using appropriate recovery tools.

∽⊙∾

Affirmation: *I continue to learn and change.*

Reflection: *What step am I working on today?*

Bend Your Knees Before You Bend Your Elbow

We prayed on the phone this morning. My struggling friend said she was "determined to stay abstinent today." I reminded her that she couldn't—but God could. So we prayed together.

Heavenly Father, keep us on the path of recovery today. Help us to say "yes" to your gift of help and healing. Help us to see that we are powerless, that without you our lives are unmanageable. Help us to remember that we have a chronic, progressive, deadly disease and that you are the solution. Your will, not ours, be done.

∽∘∾

Affirmation: *I listen for God's guidance in all of my thinking and in all of my affairs.*

Reflection: *Will I remember to ask God for a day of abstinent recovery today?*

Spirituality Is the Ability to Get Our Minds Off Ourselves

You can always spot a selfish person. You know, the selfish and self-centered to the extreme kind of person. They are usually resentful, scared, obsessed or expecting something—in other words, self-absorbed. Could that be me? Well, when we spot it, we got it! Spirituality is the ability to get our minds off ourselves.

"Relieve me of the bondage of self" through service. One of my sponsors talked a lot about service work. She did service on the lower levels, you know: world service, intergroup and region representation. I used to tease her about that. I, on the other hand, did higher-level service work: telephone calls, opening the meeting room and cleaning up afterwards, Twelve Step calls, and driving people to meetings. Whatever form our service work takes, it keeps us out of ourselves, keeps us abstinent and provides an opportunity to practice love.

Dr. Bob said that the Twelve Steps "when simmered down . . . resolve themselves into the words 'love and service.'"

∽∾

Affirmation: *Service is my gratitude in action.*

Reflection: *How will I give service today?*

Keeping Our Memories Green

Each and every food addict, abstinent or not, teaches us som valuable lessons about ourselves and recovery. We can identif with the active addict as well as with the abstinent one. The nev person and those in relapse teach us priceless lessons about the disease. They help to keep our memories green.

Where do we get these lessons? At meetings and in telephone calls. We can come away from a meeting or a phone call as a stronger person with more information about the disease and relapse process. We are reminded that if we do not work a thorough program, chances of slipping are likely.

∽○∾

Affirmation: *I learn valuable lessons from every food addict.*

Reflection: *Do I remember what it was like in the disease? What happened, and what it is like now?*

Formula for Failure: Try to Please Everyone

Please everybody, nobody's pleased;
please yourself, at least you're pleased.

Vincent P. Collins

The worst thing about people pleasing is that it is unrealistic. We cannot contrive to be what other people want us to be because what they really want is authenticity. In order to be true to ourselves and to live an authentic life, we need to examine our motives for people pleasing.

Some of the reasons we people please are the need to be liked, fear of abandonment, conflict avoidance, to gain acceptance and to make others happy. It never works! Caving in to what other people want puts our recovery in jeopardy. People have lost abstinence trying to please restaurant servers, relatives, therapists and various other people.

What can we do differently? First, we can learn to set limits. Second, we can start standing up for ourselves and our beliefs. We learn to say "no" unless saying "yes" will make us happy; *then* we say "yes." But if saying "yes" creates inconvenience and resentment, then we say "no." This process is simple but not easy. Our sponsors help us learn to set limits and find the way to put our program needs first.

∽o∾

Affirmation: *I get my needs met. I am worthy of good recovery.*

Reflection: *Am I willing to say "no" today just for the practice? How can I improve my program by prioritizing recovery?*

Let Us Write and Reflect
on the Past Week

ᢙᡐᢙ

Did I attend an adequate number of meetings?

Did I exercise too little or too much?

Did I take a Tenth Step inventory on a daily basis?

Was I accountable and honest about my food planning and implementation?

What steps did I practice?

Was I resentful, angry, selfish, dishonest or fearful?

Was I generous, kind, tolerant, patient or useful?

Were my actions, words or communications unloving or unkind?

Do I need to ask for or grant forgiveness for my actions or attitudes this week?

Was my level of hydration adequate?

Did I practice sound nutrition, including vitamins and high-quality foods?

Have I kept something to myself that should be discussed with my sponsor, advisor or therapist?

What areas of my life need improvement?

What service did I perform to help another or my group?

What was my major character flaw this week?

What was my most admirable trait this week?

Did I practice restraint of tongue and pen?

Did I rationalize any destructive behavior?

What are the corrective actions that need to be taken based on this week's inventory? Do I owe any amends?

The Path with No Obstacles
Leads Nowhere

Obstacles are a given, and overcoming them is necessary.

To overcome obstacles, we can start a research project by asking others how they dealt with the problem we face. We can check it out at meetings, ask our sponsor and—for those of us who have Internet access—join an online group of recovering people. Chances are they have met the challenges we face and will share their solutions, support and encouragement too. Self-help books are also useful sources of information.

Next, we design a plan based on the information gleaned. Then we list our aspirations and add them to our daily plan of action. Placing reminders of these new ideas in obvious places keeps them visible. Eye-catching posters are a good idea. Affirmations and visualizations put our new ideas into a positive framework and help integrate them into our lives. Next, we eliminate everything that doesn't work or support the changes we are working toward. After that, add prayer.

సంచ

Affirmation: *I easily overcome obstacles.*

Reflection: *Why not write my aspirations on a gorgeous poster and keep it in a prominent place?*

The Meaning of Life Comes from Within

I just love Michael Ryce. He says, "I am responsible for what I see, the feelings I experience, the goals I achieve, everything that happens to me, I ask for and receive!" That concept puts us squarely in charge of our own lives. And that's a fact, we are in charge of our lives.

Nothing happens to us by mistake because everything that happens to us we *ask for* and *receive*. Our thoughts create our reality.

Imagine this: We can decide to be happy. That's right; it just requires a decision!

Happiness does not depend on anything outside ourselves. It is a self-determined proposition. We can decide to be miserable too, of course, but happiness sounds like a better proposition.

So how do we take a set of circumstances and change them from messy misery to joyful harmony? We change our thinking. We learn to see things differently. So when we see a problem in the world, we fix it—when we change the way we think about it!

∽∘∾

Affirmation: *I willingly release every negative thought, attitude and belief. I see things differently now.*

Reflection: *What have I asked for? What have I received?*

Today's Stress Buster:
Practice Preventive Maintenance

For body, car, dwelling or computer, preventive maintenance can save a lot of grief.

Everything is subject to wear and tear. By undertaking a program of planned maintenance, major repair expenses can be avoided. Annual checkups are a good idea to help identify early warning signs of trouble.

Follow the experts' instructions for preventive care. That means doctor, auto manufacturer, home maintenance pro and computer expert. In recovery, preventive maintenance means using the tools before the trouble hits. Step work, meetings and following our sponsor's expert instructions pay off too!

Attainable Affirmations: Doing My Best

Affirmations are a way to let go of self-limiting beliefs. Limitations are only in our minds. We can let go of these beliefs and do our best.

∽∘∽

I give myself permission to do my best.
My best is good enough.

Only the Mind Can Lie

I'm really a very persuasive person; I can convince myself of anything. I have an addict's mind that likes to trick me.

Strange, isn't it? We are subjected to a whole list of ideas that will take us back into the disease—thoughts that will defeat and destroy us! Our job is to challenge and change self-defeating thoughts.

A friend shares, "My mind loves to tell me I am really a normal eater. I use two methods of dealing with the thoughts. I say, 'Are you crazy? Just stop that kind of thinking.' And then I change my thoughts, or I say, 'Maybe later. Not now,' and that helps me change my thought pattern. Then the thoughts go away as I get busy with something else." After we quiet those thoughts, we can turn our minds to productive things.

∽∘∾

Affirmation: I challenge and change self-defeating thoughts that threaten to take me off the path of good recovery.

Reflection: What ideas threaten my abstinence? How do I challenge those thoughts?

The Four Absolutes

When I came into recovery in 1967, the four absolutes of *honesty, unselfishness, love* and *purity* were still around but losing ground. The four absolutes were originally borrowed from the Oxford Movement by early AA members. Eventually, the absolutes practically disappeared. Not that they weren't great virtues. However, the idea of achieving absolute virtue was questionable. The concept was too compulsive for addicts. Still we can consider the advisability of striving for a high degree, an ever-increasing proficiency in the practice of these principles.

Honesty—the unending search for truth and the very foundation of our program—gets us into the program. We cannot comprehend even the first step without honesty, which is a real challenge for addicts since we are masters of deceit—deceiving both others and ourselves. We persist in our search for truth by daily inventory.

Unselfishness keeps us in the program; we can't keep it unless we give it away. We give of ourselves in order to maintain our abstinence. True unselfishness gives with no thought of reward.

Love is the spirit of the program. We learn to love God and each other—the love of one addict for another. Program love is accepting without judgment. We wish the best for each other and help each other to do our best.

Finally, we learn *purity* of mind, body and soul in order to live decent lives.

༄

Affirmation: *Each day I strive to be more honest, giving, caring and wholesome.*

Reflection: *Do I live life according to the principles of unselfishness, love, honesty and purity?*

Let Us Write and Reflect
on the Past Week

੭ॐ

Did I attend an adequate number of meetings?

Did I exercise too little or too much?

Did I take a Tenth Step inventory on a daily basis?

Was I accountable and honest about my food planning and implementation?

What steps did I practice?

Was I resentful, angry, selfish, dishonest or fearful?

Was I generous, kind, tolerant, patient or useful?

Were my actions, words or communications unloving or unkind?

Do I need to ask for or grant forgiveness for my actions or attitudes this week?

Was my level of hydration adequate?

Did I practice sound nutrition, including vitamins and high-quality foods?

Have I kept something to myself that should be discussed with my sponsor, advisor or therapist?

What areas of my life need improvement?

What service did I perform to help another or my group?

What was my major character flaw this week?

What was my most admirable trait this week?

Did I practice restraint of tongue and pen?

Did I rationalize any destructive behavior?

What are the corrective actions that need to be taken based on this week's inventory? Do I owe any amends?

Entirely Ready

In the Fifth Step, we compiled a list of character defects that we become willing to have God remove in Step Six. We become willing to let go of all of those offensive traits we have identified.

A short list of character defects are anger, criticism, dishonesty, envy, fear, gossip, hate, impatience, insincerity, jealousy, laziness, lying, negative thinking, procrastination, resentment, self-condemnation, self-justification, self-pity, selfishness and vulgarity. Are we now ready to have God remove from us these defects that keep us in emotional and spiritual turmoil?

∽∾

Affirmation: I accept and release my character defects.

Reflection: What happens when I let go of my faults? Which ones do I cling to? Why?

If You Knew Your Real Value, You Would Faint

We were all born ignorant. Along the way we were guided by people who didn't seem to know much either. No doubt, they did the best they could, but their training methods were not always enlightened. Also, we didn't learn much that was really helpful because there were lots of commands like "Don't do that" and "Because I said so"! So life was pretty much a trial-and-error effort.

Addiction took us to rock bottom with its attendant sense of failure. Then, because we are the lucky ones, we found our way into Twelve Step recovery. Here we started to get good guidance. Our sponsors may have sounded like our parents or teachers from time to time, but there was a difference. This program offered the opportunity to grow in spirit. We learned that we are good enough to do and to be our best.

We are the children of God, and as the old saying goes, "God don't make no junk!"

༺∘༻

Affirmation: *I release all thoughts of unworthiness.*

Reflection: *What keeps me from being the best I can be?*

H O P E =

Happy Our Program Exists

Remember coming out of disaster into the light of recovery? When we hit bottom, we had nowhere else to go but up.

Before our first meeting, we had reached the bottom of a downward spiral of addiction. Life was a nightmare in that descending progression. We had no idea we really had a way out. Then hope was born when we observed those in recovery who were happy, joyous and free. Watching others in the program provides the hope necessary for recovery by giving the newcomer an image for the future. That is our motivation to go forward. This week, a member said at a meeting, "It is so peaceful here because we are abstinent." It's true! We are so happy our program exists!

∽∘∾

Affirmation: I take the time to notice and be grateful for the good things coming my way.

Reflection: Do I give hope to newcomers by sharing at meetings?

Detachment

The concept of detachment—a spiritual principle—is the opposite of attachment, which is a troublemaker for sure! Practicing attachment, we give our power to outcomes, people, possessions, places and the quest for security, which creates stress, anxiety and unhappiness. In order to practice detachment, we learn to let go of the illusion that we know what is best.

Not practicing attachment with family members is tough. The first time I ever heard about the concept, which was very foreign to my thinking, was from an Al-Anon member: "Detach with love." She explained it as, "learning to detach from the alcoholic's problems and disease while still loving the person."

Kahlil Gibran teaches detachment from our children saying, "Though they are with you yet they belong not to you. You may give them your love but not your thoughts. For they have their own thoughts." That's a tough order—to allow our children their own lives and ideas, success and failures.

Detachment is freedom from knowing best!

∽∘∾

Affirmation: I do the footwork and give the results to a Greater Intelligence.

Reflection: How do I detach from outcomes? Am I able to put it all in God's hands?

Peace Be with You

*There is a place in you where
there is perfect peace.*

A Course in Miracles, p. 76.

Life can be chaotic. Occasionally, we feel happy or content or peaceful. However, that feeling is hard to maintain. Conflict happens! We feel empty, afraid and frustrated. Take heart, a solution to our discordant lives is available.

True peace is not the absence of distress; it is a state of mind. When we maintain an outlook of love and acceptance, we enjoy serenity and peace of mind. We focus on that place in us where there is perfect peace—the "peace which surpasses all understanding" —which comes from God to us through our spiritual practices.

In the program, we call this peaceful state "serenity." God is its source. When we live in God's world of love and acceptance, we experience the harmonious lives we seek. The Twelve Steps are our pathway to true peace.

༄

Affirmation: I am at peace with myself and in harmony with those around me.

Reflection: What disrupts my peace and happiness? When disturbed, how can I regain serenity?

Pity Pot

Self-pity is choosing helplessness and victimhood. *Look what happened to me! Poor me, poor me!*

When unacceptable things happen, we feel sorry for ourselves. Feeling sorry for ourselves needn't be a way of life. Eventually, it becomes nauseating, stomach turning and unbearable. Self-pity creates misery for ourselves and those who are forced to interact with us. It can lead to depression and despair.

D. H. Lawrence writes these stunning words about self-pity: "I never saw a wild thing sorry for itself. A small bird will drop frozen dead from a bough without ever having felt sorry for itself."

Self-pity is a human thing. When it is the product of self-absorption, we drown in it. Self-pity is born out of expectations. We get so caught up in thinking about ourselves that we stop seeking God's will and are no longer useful to others.

The way out is to process and express our feelings of disappointment and disillusionment and to move on. We pray to be relieved of bondage of self. We abandon ourselves to God and to God's work, seeking only God's will for us and the power to carry it out. It's a relief!

∽◦∽

Affirmation: *I know that great lessons come from disappointments.*

Reflection: *Do I accept my successes and failures equally as learning opportunities?*

Let Us Write and Reflect
on the Past Week

ౚఞ

Did I attend an adequate number of meetings?

Did I exercise too little or too much?

Did I take a Tenth Step inventory on a daily basis?

Was I accountable and honest about my food planning and implementation?

What steps did I practice?

Was I resentful, angry, selfish, dishonest or fearful?

Was I generous, kind, tolerant, patient or useful?

Were my actions, words or communications unloving or unkind?

Do I need to ask for or grant forgiveness for my actions or attitudes this week?

Was my level of hydration adequate?

Did I practice sound nutrition, including vitamins and high-quality foods?

Have I kept something to myself that should be discussed with my sponsor, advisor or therapist?

What areas of my life need improvement?

What service did I perform to help another or my group?

What was my major character flaw this week?

What was my most admirable trait this week?

Did I practice restraint of tongue and pen?

Did I rationalize any destructive behavior?

What are the corrective actions that need to be taken based on this week's inventory? Do I owe any amends?

The Twelve Steps are the spiritual principles that guide us in our personal recovery. The founders of AA came up with twelve principles—Traditions—that keep our groups intact. These Twelve Traditions are to the groups what the Twelve Steps are to the individual. They are suggested principles that ensure the survival and growth of the group. Hammered out on the anvil of experience, they were designed to guide our groups. Personal survival and survival of our program depend on understanding and implementing these principles. We need to develop a personal regard for the Twelve Traditions and an awareness of our role in preserving the unity of our Twelve Step program. In recovery, we become practitioners of the Twelve Steps *and* the Twelve Traditions.

TRADITION SIX

"A group ought never endorse, finance, or lend the fellowship's name to any related facility or outside enterprise, lest problems of money, property, and prestige divert us from our primary purpose."

The program is spiritual. The Sixth Tradition separates the spiritual from the material. The fellowship is not a money maker and is not interested in wealth or gain or the problems that materialism generates. A meeting place to share our message and a "prudent reserve" to meet the financial needs of our groups is all we need. We do not lend our name to "outside enterprises," we do not own property, nor do we seek to do so. On a personal level, we guard against making announcements concerning nonprogram enterprises at meetings. We attend business meetings where the use of our funds is discussed and voted upon. We never use our program contacts, meeting lists and phone numbers for personal gain. Finally, we support the use of conference-approved literature at our meetings.

∽∘∾

Affirmation: *I focus on my group's primary purpose to carry the message of recovery.*

Reflection: *Do I avoid any mention of "outside enterprises" in our meetings?*

Adjustment to Life

One of the delights of recovery is that we can stop banging our heads against the brick wall of life. Metaphorically and realistically, the headaches will stop.

We learn to live life on life's terms, which contrasts with the self-will riot that we experienced throughout the addicted years. We get tools to help us calm down and adjust to life. It happens gradually as we grow and learn. Acceptance is needed to deal with life on life's terms. The promise in the AA book comes true, ". . . we have ceased fighting anything or anyone. . . ."

The daily inventory question to ask is, "What am I fighting today?" The answer tells me exactly what my acceptance work is for today: Can I change it? If yes, then change it. Can I change it? If no, then accept it!

∽∘∾

Affirmation: Acceptance is the answer to my discord today.

Reflection: Do I work on acceptance by taking a quick-check inventory when irritated or disturbed? What am I fighting today?

Resigning from the Debating Society

"We don't debate, we recover." There is real confidence in that statement. It says, there is nothing left to debate. When we find the effective way to get abstinent and stay abstinent, there is nothing to disagree about.

We know when we have found the right way for us. Accepting others' views as right for them is part of our recovery path. We never argue, everyone must decide for themselves.

Although we are always open to new information, no one has demonstrated the value of eating sugar, flour or wheat. Just the opposite! We talk to people every day who have tried that way with its bitter consequences. We don't want what they have. There is no argument, no experimentation left when we find the clean, abstinent way of life.

∽o∾

Affirmation: I enjoy a recovery process with reliable results.

Reflection: Have I accepted clean, weighed and measured abstinence as my way of life? Do I have the confidence to say, "I don't debate, I recover"?

Hurry and Indecision

Just for today, I will have a program.
I may not follow it exactly, but I will have it,
thereby saving myself from two pests:
hurry and indecision.

Having trouble making up our minds is a damaging force, leaving us with problems unsolved and work undone while we waste time and energy trying to decide what to do. On the other hand, when we are in the hurry mode, we tear about frustrated and nervous, working too hard, driving too fast, rushing from place to place.

The solution is to have a realistic program—one that is achievable. The AA book has just the approach:

In thinking about our day we may face indecision.
We may not be able to determine which course to take.
Here we ask God for inspiration, an intuitive thought or a
decision. We relax and take it easy. We don't struggle.
We are often surprised how the right answers come
after we have tried this for a while.

❧

Affirmation: *I have a plan. I ask God for inspiration. I relax and practice "easy does it."*

Reflection: *Is planning part of my recovery program? How does failure to plan affect my abstinence?*

The Promises

"If we are painstaking about this phase of our development, we will be amazed before we are halfway through. We are going to know a new freedom and a new happiness. We will not regret the past, nor wish to shut the door on it. We will comprehend the word serenity and we will know peace. No matter how far down the scale we have gone, we will see how our experience can benefit others. That feeling of uselessness and self-pity will disappear. We will lose interest in selfish things and gain interest in our fellows. Self-seeking will slip away. Our whole attitude and outlook upon life will change. Fear of people and of economic insecurity will leave us. We will intuitively know how to handle situations that used to baffle us. We will suddenly realize that God is doing for us what we could not do for ourselves.

Are these extravagant promises? We think not. They are being fulfilled among us—sometimes quickly, sometimes slowly. They will always materialize if we work for them."

Alcoholics Anonymous, p. 83-84

∽o∽

Affirmation: God's gifts overcome all limitations.

Reflection: How are the recovery promises being demonstrated in my life?

Think God!

Are you familiar with the golden key? Emmet Fox describes a method of problem solving that is "simplicity itself. All you have to do is this: *Stop thinking about the difficulty whatever it is, and think about God instead.*" That is the golden key to problem solving.

Think God! Whenever a disturbing thought arises—think about God instead. Each time a troublesome relationship comes to mind—recite the attributes of God. Speak everything you believe about him: God is peace, power, mercy, light, love, goodness, understanding, intelligence and so on. This is the way to "let go and let God!"

❦

Affirmation: I think of God during any threat or challenge to my serenity that develops.

Reflection: How might thinking of God help me through difficult times? Has this worked for me in the past?

Let Us Write and Reflect
on the Past Week

～⌘～

Did I attend an adequate number of meetings?

Did I exercise too little or too much?

Did I take a Tenth Step inventory on a daily basis?

Was I accountable and honest about my food planning and implementation?

What steps did I practice?

Was I resentful, angry, selfish, dishonest or fearful?

Was I generous, kind, tolerant, patient or useful?

Were my actions, words or communications unloving or unkind?

Do I need to ask for or grant forgiveness for my actions or attitudes this week?

Was my level of hydration adequate?

Did I practice sound nutrition, including vitamins and high-quality foods?

Have I kept something to myself that should be discussed with my sponsor, advisor or therapist?

What areas of my life need improvement?

What service did I perform to help another or my group?

What was my major character flaw this week?

What was my most admirable trait this week?

Did I practice restraint of tongue and pen?

Did I rationalize any destructive behavior?

What are the corrective actions that need to be taken based on this week's inventory? Do I owe any amends?

Let Us Write and Reflect on
the Following Questions

∞∞

How do I waste time? What can I do differently?

_____

_____

_____

_____

_____

_____

_____

_____

_____

_____

_____

_____

_____

_____

_____

_____

_____

Life on Life's Terms

Let's remind ourselves of this reality: Just putting down our substances does not exempt us from life's challenges. We learn to face life on life's terms.

Life's challenges keep us growing. As we grow in recovery, we begin to realize that it is not so much what happens to us in life but how we handle it. We can find peace within any storm with the help of our Higher Power, our support system and practicing the Twelve Steps.

A friend shares, "Just because I am committed to my recovery and work hard at my program, I am not exempt from life's difficulties and problems. Because of my connection to God and to my recovery community, I handle those things with less stress and fear. With recovery, I have found peace within the storm."

∽o∽

Affirmation: I see life's difficulties as opportunities from God for me to grow.

Reflection: How do I use my program tools of literature, sponsorship and the telephone to find solutions to situations that used to baffle me?

Let Us Write and Reflect
on the Following Idea

∽∘∽

Every time we say "I must do something," it takes an incredible amount of energy. Far more than physically doing it.

Gita Bellin

Start from Where You Stand

No one can go back and make a brand-new start. Anyone can start from now and make a brand-new ending.

No matter what the blunder—a missed opportunity, an outrageous loss of control or a bad decision—we cannot change the past. Often we tend to dwell on it, feeling guilty and afraid. What do we do with the past? Well, since we can't just dismiss it and don't want to dwell on it, we can learn from it.

The Big Book says, "We will not regret the past nor wish to shut the door on it." Our history of destructive behaviors and attendant consequences brought us to the meeting room doors. In those rooms, and with the recovering people we find there, we learn from our past mistakes.

We use the past to grow spiritually. We come to view life as in this prayer: "Oh Lord, I'm not what I ought to be—I'm not what I want to be—I'm not what I'm going to be—but oh Lord, I thank you that I'm not what I used to be."

∽∘∾

Affirmation: I use the past to learn how to grow today.

Reflection: What does this past behavior say about me? What changes do I need to make right now?

Laughter

When I do Humor and Play workshops, I spend a lot of time laughing and giggling while preparing the program. I feel so great on those days!

Laughter makes me feel good all over. Isn't it fun to watch healthy little ones laugh and smile? Laughter provides their growing minds and bodies with vital stimulation and exercise. And for people of all ages, laughter is good for health. It is a great stress reliever, combats disease and might even help us live longer.

Laughter is aerobic too! It increases our supply of oxygen. Try the ho-ho-ha-ha exercise: My friend Margot taught me how to laugh without any reason. It is fun to do in a group. Together we chant ho-ho ha-ha while clapping our hands once on each ho and ha. This activity gets us laughing for sure. Whole groups of us respond to this exercise with hoots and cheers.

∽∘∾

Affirmation: I make a healthy choice to have laugh time.

Reflection: Why not make a list of things that cause me to laugh and make hilarity part of my recovery program?

The Stages of Surrender

Surrender takes place in stages. First we surrender to the fact of our addiction. Then we surrender to a course of action prescribed by others. In this stage, surrender means being willing to follow someone's else's direction.

Remember what happened when we followed our own course? Our best thinking got us in a whole lot of trouble because of our infinite ability to deceive ourselves. Self-deception obscures the real nature of our problems, and because of that, most of the solutions we conjure up will make matters worse. That is why we need clear-thinking, objective outsiders.

A friend shares, "Surrender sets my cruise control for recovery. I have my plan and I've turned over the specifics to my sponsor." Where does our plan of action originate? From recovery literature, discussion meetings and sponsors. From there on, we follow our directions in order to surrender our will to our Higher Power.

ఒం

Affirmation: I seek the wise counsel of my sponsor.

Reflection: Am I willing to follow directions from those who have what I want?

Let Us Write and Reflect
on the Past Week

༺ঔ৹

Did I attend an adequate number of meetings?

Did I exercise too little or too much?

Did I take a Tenth Step inventory on a daily basis?

Was I accountable and honest about my food planning and implementation?

What steps did I practice?

Was I resentful, angry, selfish, dishonest or fearful?

Was I generous, kind, tolerant, patient or useful?

Were my actions, words or communications unloving or unkind?

Do I need to ask for or grant forgiveness for my actions or attitudes this week?

Was my level of hydration adequate?

Did I practice sound nutrition, including vitamins and high-quality foods?

Have I kept something to myself that should be discussed with my sponsor, advisor or therapist?

What areas of my life need improvement?

What service did I perform to help another or my group?

What was my major character flaw this week?

What was my most admirable trait this week?

Did I practice restraint of tongue and pen?

Did I rationalize any destructive behavior?

What are the corrective actions that need to be taken based on this week's inventory? Do I owe any amends?

If Love Is Not the Answer,
Then I Misunderstood the Question

Applying the "love answer" to every question is a real challenge. When I talked to my friend yesterday, we talked about three painful situations in her life. Love was lacking in every one of them. She believed that three of her relatives were causing her problems. Like a lawyer arguing a case, she made them all look pretty bad. However, the real problem was lack of love. She thought that her relatives were responsible for her happiness. She believed that if those three would cooperate and respect her wishes, she would be happy.

What was her real problem? A mistaken goal. She made cooperation and respect from others more important than her personal power and her spiritual condition.

Whenever we place expectations on others, we are rehearsing for a resentment. Folks are not going to act the way we think they *should*. When she put those shoulds on her relatives, she gave them her power. She made them responsible for her well-being. She traded love for anger. When she became willing to give up her expectations, drop the criticism and take responsibility for her behavior and emotions, she was able to return to a peaceful and loving place with her family members.

✧

Affirmation: *Today I eliminate the shoulds!*

Reflection: *Do I take responsibility for my angry feelings, or do I expect others to act in a way that will make me happy?*

There Is One Who Has All Power

Anything we love more than God becomes our idol—a false god.

In addiction, food slowly becomes our god as our lives revolve more and more around it. All the experiences of life—holidays, vacations, time off, trips, relationships and daily life—are planned with a view toward the food that is served. Gradually, we start focusing on food more than anything else. Food takes over. We think about it obsessively, we eat it compulsively. We are powerless.

Then we discover the solution: the power of the real God! Once we enter into a relationship with the God of Abstinence, we will be set free.

∽∘∾

Affirmation: I have found the One who has all Power.

Reflection: Have I asked God to stand between food and me so that food will not stand between God and me?

It's a Pity We Can't Forget Our Troubles the Way We Forget Our Blessings

We have built-in "forgetters" for so many things. Why is memory so short for the blessings in our lives and so long when it comes to resentment, pain and worry?

Gratitude lists are such a good idea. That's why I have little sheets to remind me to list my blessings.

∽∽∽

Affirmation: *My attitude is gratitude.*

Reflection: *Today I will write down at least ten things for which I am grateful.*

Facing Fear

Sometimes we think fear ought to be classed with stealing.
It seems to cause more trouble. We reviewed our fears
thoroughly. We put them on paper, even though we had no
resentment in connection with them. We asked ourselves
why we had them. Wasn't it because self-reliance failed us?

Alcoholics Anonymous, p. 67-68

Admitting that we are filled with fear takes a lot of courage. Often we bluff our way through life, ignoring and hiding the fact that we are scared. We hide it even from ourselves.

An important principle of recovery is taking inventory. As the AA book suggests, we set our fears down on paper. What a terrifying task! This may be the first time we have even a nodding acquaintance with fear. Inventory is the beginning of owning these feelings. Once we enumerate and examine our fears they begin to lose power.

Since self-reliance has failed us, it takes a leap of faith to trust God to keep us safe. At first we are like the man who fell off the mountain. He grabbed on to a little tree and held on for dear life. He started yelling, "Is there anyone up there who can help me?" A powerful voice answered him, "Let go!" The fallen man yelled back, "Is there anybody else up there?"

Trust is a leap of faith; we let go and jump. Self-reliance has failed us; reliance on God must be the answer. There are no guarantees, we just jump.

∽◦∾

Affirmation: *I trust God to care for me.*

Reflection: *Do I trust God to keep me safe?*

Today's Stress Buster:
Say "No" More Often

Being a "yes man" is so darn easy. We want to rush in to fix, help or rescue. It feels great to be cooperative and helpful—until life spins out of control. Saying "no" puts us in charge rather than giving power to those who seek our help.

Practice saying "no" just to get the hang of it. Try the graceful no-nonsense approach: "Thanks for thinking of me. I must say no this time." No excuses are necessary.

Attainable Affirmations:
Healthy Way

Affirmations are a powerful way for training the mind to focus on health and happiness as a way of life.

∽o∾

I meet the day feeling happy, healthy, loving and alive.

I willingly accept health and happiness.

Let Us Write and Reflect
on the Past Week

ᔓᔕᔕ

Did I attend an adequate number of meetings?

Did I exercise too little or too much?

Did I take a Tenth Step inventory on a daily basis?

Was I accountable and honest about my food planning and implementation?

What steps did I practice?

Was I resentful, angry, selfish, dishonest or fearful?

Was I generous, kind, tolerant, patient or useful?

Were my actions, words or communications unloving or unkind?

Do I need to ask for or grant forgiveness for my actions or attitudes this week?

Was my level of hydration adequate?

Did I practice sound nutrition, including vitamins and high-quality foods?

Have I kept something to myself that should be discussed with my sponsor, advisor or therapist?

What areas of my life need improvement?

What service did I perform to help another or my group?

What was my major character flaw this week?

What was my most admirable trait this week?

Did I practice restraint of tongue and pen?

Did I rationalize any destructive behavior?

What are the corrective actions that need to be taken based on this week's inventory? Do I owe any amends?

Slogans Are Wisdom Written in Shorthand

First Things First
Easy Does It
Live and Let Live
But for the Grace of God
One Day at a Time
This, Too, Shall Pass
Let Go and Let God
Stick with the Winners
Keep It Simple

Life gets confusing and complicated at times. Sometimes a simple idea can put us back on track. That's why slogans, uttered by sponsors and heard at meetings, are tacked up in meeting rooms. They seem simplistic, but behind those simple words lie sound recovery wisdom. Having slogans pasted around our homes and autos as recovery reminders might be a good idea.

∽✧∾

Affirmation: *I find deeper meaning behind each recovery slogan.*

Reflection: *Do I use the simple slogans to help me in complicated situations?*

Humbly Asked Him...

The practice of the steps certainly helps to reduce our inflated egos in order to discover a more realistic sense of ourselves. My favorite definition is, "Humility is not thinking less of yourself, but thinking of yourself less." In Step Seven, *"we humbly ask God to remove our shortcomings."* With these words, we open ourselves to the grace and power of God.

∽∘∾

Affirmation: *I recognize my character defects, and I ask God to remove them.*

Reflection: *What is the Step Seven method of dealing with shortcomings? How is it different from ways I have tried in the past?*

Let Freedom Ring

Free to eat sweets, treats and baked goods? Sure we are. Free to say no to those refined and processed foods? Only if we have clean abstinence.

Once we commit to sugar, the sugar takes over. To the diseased mind, it seems the opposite. Those who say no seem to lack choice. However, clean abstinence is the only condition that allows free choice. To have a choice indicates the possibility of two or more options. Addiction allows one—a commitment to gorging with all its consequences.

In abstinence, I am free to be the person I was meant to be.

The gifts of abstinence are . . .

Freedom from craving
Freedom from obsession and compulsion
Freedom from isolation
Freedom from guilty eating and sneaking
Freedom from fear, shame and hopelessness
Freedom from weight-loss programs
Freedom from stagnation.

❧

Affirmation: *I enjoy my freedom with gratitude.*

Reflection: *Did addictive food offer me any freedom at all, or did it condemn me to a life of gorging?*

We're Responsible for the Effort,
Not the Outcome

A friend shares,

I am having one of those days where I have too much to do. Just the thought of it makes me feel uncomfortable. I am haunted by all kinds of fear—fear of failure, fear of not being good enough, fear of not living up to other people's expectations, fear of not being exceptional and, above all, fear of not being perfect. That darn perfectionism is an outstanding contributor to my disease. It causes a lot of discomfort in my life. Why can I not just settle for good? I have a lot of recovery in this area. Sometimes I mistakenly believe that I am recovered from perfection addiction, but even in this area it is "progress not perfection."

Perfectionism should appear on our list of character defects. Perfectionists set unrealistically high goals. These attempts end in failure resulting in guilt, anxiety and depression. The pressure is always on to perform.

Progress, not perfection. What comforting words. The idea of progress puts the focus on the process, not the outcome. Focusing on the activity keeps us in the present. We wash dishes in order to wash dishes. No perfection required. We just do it to do it. Nothing else is required—not even really clean dishes.

∽∘∾

Affirmation: *My best is good enough! I value the mistakes that help me learn and grow.*

Reflection: *Have I ever honored failure? Today I will identify a recent mistake and list everything I learned from it.*

Recovery Delivers Everything Binge Food Promised

We ate for happiness and became unhappy.

We ate for joy and became miserable.

We ate to be outgoing and became self-centered.

We ate for sociability and became argumentative.

We ate to be agreeable and became irritable.

We ate for friendship and made enemies.

We ate to sleep and awakened without rest.

We ate for strength and felt weak.

We ate for energy and became apathetic.

We ate for relaxation and got edgy.

We ate for confidence and were filled with doubt.

We ate for freedom and became slaves.

We ate for power and were powerless.

We ate to soften sorrow and wallowed in self-pity.

We ate medicinally and acquired health problems.

We ate because the job called for it and lost the job.

We ate to feel heavenly and knew hell.

We ate to forget and were haunted.

We ate to handle problems and saw them multiply.

We ate to cope with life and invited death.

We ate to feel better and always felt worse.

∽○∽

Affirmation: *I find happiness and contentment in recovery.*

Reflection: *Have I learned that everything I lost in the disease can be found in recovery?*

Pride Goeth Before the Fall

"Pride" is a funny word because it can mean something detrimental such as being vain and haughty. On the other hand, we think of taking *pride* in a job well done, and that's a good thing. Take note, however, that pride appears on the list of the seven deadly sins, which puts it right up there with the most dangerous of shortcomings.

So how do we discover the treacherous form of pride in our personality? The Twelve Steps make us aware of the egomaniac within—our inflated ego. Unchecked, that ego will take us swiftly back into the disease. In modern terms, ego goeth before the relapse.

Through the use of the steps, we learn genuine humility, which has nothing to do with humiliation. Nothing in the steps requires us to dishonor ourselves. Living the Twelve Step way of life, we experience ego deflation in order to establish a realistic sense of ourselves.

The Seventh Step is where we make the change in our attitude which permits us, with humility as our guide, to move out from ourselves toward others and toward God.

A.A. *Twelve Steps and Twelve Traditions*, p. 76

∽∘∾

Affirmation: *Today I experience more of God and less of me.*

Reflection: *What are the attributes of humility? How can I strive to practice humility?*

Let Us Write and Reflect
on the Past Week

༚〜༚

Did I attend an adequate number of meetings?

Did I exercise too little or too much?

Did I take a Tenth Step inventory on a daily basis?

Was I accountable and honest about my food planning and implementation?

What steps did I practice?

Was I resentful, angry, selfish, dishonest or fearful?

Was I generous, kind, tolerant, patient or useful?

Were my actions, words or communications unloving or unkind?

Do I need to ask for or grant forgiveness for my actions or attitudes this week?

Was my level of hydration adequate?

Did I practice sound nutrition, including vitamins and high-quality foods?

Have I kept something to myself that should be discussed with my sponsor, advisor or therapist?

What areas of my life need improvement?

What service did I perform to help another or my group?

What was my major character flaw this week?

What was my most admirable trait this week?

Did I practice restraint of tongue and pen?

Did I rationalize any destructive behavior?

What are the corrective actions that need to be taken based on this week's inventory? Do I owe any amends?

I Can't Do God's Will My Way

To let go is to let go of self-will and the desire to control and manage all things and everyone. We do this in order to let God operate in our lives.

Step One showed us that our lives had become unmanageable. We need better supervision. Letting go does not give us the license to start ignoring responsibilities, to do nothing, to sit back and wait for miracles, or to make no decisions. Instead our job is to do the possible and let God take care of the impossible.

We start by raising our awareness of those times when we try to force a result, make something happen or attempt to change a situation or a person. Then it is time to let go and let God. Sometimes we do this in desperation with a prayer giving our struggle to our Higher Power: "Take this and change me, I cannot go on like this." When we give up the struggle, frustration is replaced with peace.

∾ஐ∾

Affirmation: *I let go and let God.*

Reflection: *Today I will write my struggles, worries and complaints on a piece of paper and place them in a God box, saying, "Your will, not mine, be done."*

The Twelve Steps are the spiritual principles that guide us in our personal recovery. The founders of AA came up with twelve principles—Traditions—that keep our groups intact. These Twelve Traditions are to the groups what the Twelve Steps are to the individual. They are suggested principles that ensure the survival and growth of the group. Hammered out on the anvil of experience, they were designed to guide our groups. Personal survival and survival of our program depend on understanding and implementing these principles. We need to develop a personal regard for the Twelve Traditions and an awareness of our role in preserving the unity of our Twelve Step program. In recovery, we become practitioners of the Twelve Steps *and* the Twelve Traditions.

TRADITION SEVEN

*"Every group ought to be fully self-supporting,
declining outside contributions."*

Our groups pay their way. In order to do that, we the members pay our way too. Outside contributions are refused. Not even the donation of a meeting place is accepted because groups are responsible to pay reasonable rent for their meeting space. In order to avoid controversy, large donations are refused. When the basket is passed, members contribute to the best of their ability. On a personal level, we support our group, intergroup and international service office by our voluntary contributions. If we can afford it, at least a two-dollar contribution per meeting is suggested.

∽∘∾

Affirmation: I willingly contribute my fair share when the basket is passed.

Reflection: How can I help my group become self-supporting?

God Is Always on Time

God is never early, God is never late. He is always timely and always in charge. We can count on that. He knows our needs and meets them, even though God might not operate on our time schedule. Have you ever prayed, "Thanks God for getting the job done. I had hoped it would be a year ago, because then I wouldn't have worried so much"?

We surely do not know the mind of God, but we can guess that God might have many reasons for saying, "Not now!" I suspect usually the lesson is in the waiting.

I recently received a message from a friend whose daughter suffered through a series of trying situations while getting a divorce. It seemed that her problems would never resolve. My friend said,

> *I have been worried sick that she would have a break-down or turn to alcohol through all this. I have been praying so hard that it would be resolved on December twentieth as scheduled. I tried to turn it over to God, I knew that she was in His care, and yet I held on to the worry and fear. When she didn't telephone on the twentieth, I thought it was because she couldn't bear to tell me the bad news. Well, she telephoned yesterday and everything went well. Now she is preparing to start a new life. I am so grateful and happy for her and grateful that I didn't lose my abstinence over all this.*

Even when God is right on time, we can choose to worry right up to the deadline. The lesson here? Worry puts us in a bad place spiritually. "An anxious heart weighs a man down" (Prov. 12:25). The spiritual implications of worry are significant. When we worry, we demonstrate mistrust. Worry tells God that we don't believe He will love and care for us. Certainly, learning belief and trust takes practice so that we can return to joyful living. Worry doesn't prevent disaster; it prevents joy.

∽∘∽

Affirmation: I believe that I am safe in God's care and assured of His love.

Reflection: Do I pray and trust or worry and fuss? How can I pray more and worry less?

Commitment to What?

Recently I was objectively looking at an addictive food. There was no longing in my glance because I am happily abstinent. The thought crossed my mind as I glimpsed that particular food: *If I were to eat that, I would be making a commitment to chewing. Nonstop chewing.*

Yep, that's how addiction works for me. Once I start, I just keep on chewing. There is no stopping me. There is no off button. Just ceaseless chewing. Hand to mouth, on and on. There is no tasting, no enjoyment, just working those teeth until I pass out. My jaw started to ache, just thinking about it.

Picking up that stuff would result in more than an aching jaw. Every part of my being—body, mind and spirit—would ache. Nope, no pain-producing foods for me today.

∽∽

Affirmation: I practice unconditional abstinence every day.

Reflection: How do I deviate from unconditional abstinence? How can these deviations be remedied?

Make Your Course Regular

Consistency is a quality that contributes to excellent recovery. We can't stay abstinent on yesterday's program. Our disease is current, and our efforts must be up-to-date too. When we let down our guard, the disease takes advantage.

A friend recently went to a new restaurant, but her order was too casual to sustain abstinence. She paid the price with a bad headache and renewed struggle to obtain and maintain abstinence.

Casual recovery doesn't work. Recovery disciplines must be consistent. When we are constant, people know what to expect from us. Consistency shows that we are serious about our program; then those around us take it seriously too.

∽∾∽

Affirmation: *Today I perform the recovery tasks that worked yesterday.*

Reflection: *Specifically, what results have I achieved from inconsistent recovery practices? How can casual recovery be corrected?*

Self-Respect

A friend was speaking of a close relative for whom she had no respect. "He doesn't deserve it," she says. What does this comment say about her relative? Nothing! What does it say about her? That she is disrespectful.

What others deserve is not the point. No one needs to earn our respect. We show respect because we choose to be respectful. To be otherwise would allow someone else to determine our level of spirituality. Our job is not to determine who deserves good treatment. What we ourselves deserve is to be our most respectful, loving best.

The outside world always provides excuses for us to be unprincipled. When we choose a spiritual way of life, however, certain principles apply. Respect for others is a spiritual principle, and when we choose to live a spiritual way of life we show respect to others.

∞

Affirmation: *I am respectful of others.*

Reflection: *In what ways am I disrespectful? Am I willing to make amends when I show disrespect to others?*

Let Us Write and Reflect
on the Past Week

ᴄᴏᴏ

Did I attend an adequate number of meetings?

Did I exercise too little or too much?

Did I take a Tenth Step inventory on a daily basis?

Was I accountable and honest about my food planning and implementation?

What steps did I practice?

Was I resentful, angry, selfish, dishonest or fearful?

Was I generous, kind, tolerant, patient or useful?

Were my actions, words or communications unloving or unkind?

Do I need to ask for or grant forgiveness for my actions or attitudes this week?

Was my level of hydration adequate?

Did I practice sound nutrition, including vitamins and high-quality foods?

Have I kept something to myself that should be discussed with my sponsor, advisor or therapist?

What areas of my life need improvement?

What service did I perform to help another or my group?

What was my major character flaw this week?

What was my most admirable trait this week?

Did I practice restraint of tongue and pen?

Did I rationalize any destructive behavior?

What are the corrective actions that need to be taken based on this week's inventory? Do I owe any amends?

Smile, You Are in Recovery

"But we aren't a glum lot.
If newcomers could see no joy or fun
in our existence, they wouldn't want it.
We absolutely insist on
enjoying life."

Alcoholics Anonymous, p. 132

We were laughing so hard at the meeting last night when the remark was made, "We wouldn't be having this much fun if we were into food and drugs." Hey, wait a minute! That's why we were doing the food, drink and drugs, wasn't it? To have fun? Looks like it didn't work.

Let's face it, addiction is no fun at all. And to think, we wondered what we would do for enjoyment when we got sober and abstinent. That is what we did to have fun—got sober and abstinent.

∽◦∽

Affirmation: I am happy, joyous and free.

Reflection: What shall I do today to bring more joy into my life?

Let Us Write and Reflect on
the Following Question

∽∽

For what problems am I searching for solutions?

_____

_____

_____

_____

_____

_____

_____

_____

_____

_____

_____

_____

_____

_____

_____

I Am Worthy of Lasting Recovery

Yo-yo dieters may become zero-one abstainers. The yo-yo diet syndrome is typified by dieting, losing weight, returning to addictive eating, gaining weight, finding a new diet, losing weight and on and on. As a yo-yo goes up and down, weight goes up and down for those who live this nightmare of addictive disease.

When we get into recovery, we sometimes fear that we will meet with the same "success followed by failure" syndrome. Recovery is different. When we really apply ourselves to the recovery process, we aim to maintain lasting abstinence coupled with progressive growth. However, we need to guard against the zero-one pattern. That is the pattern by which we get abstinent, complete withdrawals, lose it, eat addictively, and return again and again to abstinence, withdrawal and relapse. Life in this process is fraught with pain—the pain of withdrawal, the pain of disease.

Getting abstinent requires a lot of effort. To stay abstinent, we need to continue to apply ourselves to the tasks of recovery. We deserve lasting recovery. We achieve this by perseverance. Continued effort brings results.

∽○∽

Affirmation: *I am steadfast in my purpose to maintain lasting recovery.*

Reflection: *Today I will sustain recovery by using the tools that work: meetings, step work, sponsor contact, phone calls, reading, writing, prayer and meditation.*

The Urge Surge

Every addict has felt the urge surge—you know, those times when an enormous surge of desire for binge food overtakes us. This surge is one of those cunning, baffling and powerful times. Sometimes the urge follows a strong memory of past experiences with binge food: holiday foods, eating in the car, passing a poison palace (binge food store) . . . any of these might bring up the desire to eat in the old way.

The AA book on page 43 says, "The alcoholic at certain times has no effective mental defense against the first drink. Except in a few cases, neither he nor any other human being can provide such a defense. His defense must come from a Higher Power."

The same is true for the food addict; we have no effective mental defense or technique that will turn us away from the first bite. This defense must come from a Higher Power. The Twelve Steps are our guide to this Power.

∽o∾

Affirmation: I invoke my Higher Power's protection when the urge to eat strikes.

Reflection: Have I admitted and accepted that no mental defense exists against the first bite? Have I sought my Higher Power's protection in times of great temptation?

Let Us Write and Reflect on
the Following Idea

༦◦◦

Until one is committed, there is hesitancy, the chance to draw back, always ineffectiveness . . . the moment one definitely commits oneself, then Providence moves too.

The Scottish Himalayan Expedition

First Things First

My old sponsor would say, "If I put first things first, what comes second?" I am pretty sure recovery won't take second place. It takes first place or no place at all.

Violating this law of recovery pays off in extreme anguish. We face such a dilemma trying to figure out how to pull this off. We need a plan—one that provides just the right amount of recovery activity for maintenance and growth. On the other hand, we must guard against overdoing. This seems pretty tricky: asking an addict to be moderate. Certainly, since we can't stay abstinent on yesterday's program, we need certain recovery activities every day—others on a weekly, monthly and annual basis.

ᢍᠥᢋ

Affirmation: Daily recovery is my goal. I do first things first.

Reflection: Have I identified my personal daily, weekly, monthly and annual requirements for recovery?

Let Us Write and Reflect
on the Past Week

Did I attend an adequate number of meetings?

Did I exercise too little or too much?

Did I take a Tenth Step inventory on a daily basis?

Was I accountable and honest about my food planning and implementation?

What steps did I practice?

Was I resentful, angry, selfish, dishonest or fearful?

Was I generous, kind, tolerant, patient or useful?

Were my actions, words or communications unloving or unkind?

Do I need to ask for or grant forgiveness for my actions or attitudes this week?

Was my level of hydration adequate?

Did I practice sound nutrition, including vitamins and high-quallty foods?

Have I kept something to myself that should be discussed with my sponsor, advisor or therapist?

What areas of my life need improvement?

What service did I perform to help another or my group?

What was my major character flaw this week?

What was my most admirable tralt this week?

Did I practice restraint of tongue and pen?

Did I rationalize any destructive behavior?

What are the corrective actions that need to be taken based on this week's inventory? Do I owe any amends?

Lean on Me

What is a friend? It is someone with whom you dare to be yourself.

I have a special friend, and today I want to share about her. We have a friendship born out of the fellowship. We trust each other with our deepest concerns and hopes. My friend and I get together regularly. We have a meal and catch up on each other's lives. My friend is genuine. With her, what you see is what you get—no artifice.

So it was to this friend that I confided when I faced my toughest life challenge. Not only did she understand, encourage and comfort me, she packed her bags and traveled across the continent with me to support me in my most terrifying hour. This lady demonstrates all the qualities of a true friend. She is someone you can lean on.

⌀⌀

Affirmation: I pray to be a good friend.

Reflection: Today I will take a "friendship inventory" to see if I am trustworthy, supportive, loyal, understanding, empathetic and honest with my friends.

Accepting the Things I Cannot Change

The power of this idea is beyond description. All change begins with recognition, admission and acceptance. To be spiritually fit, emotionally healthy and at peace, we must learn the acceptance lesson. We usually ask, "But what about the unacceptable?" The hardest work of all is to learn to give up our stance on any subject in order to feel peace.

We will never be at peace if we wait for the world to change. We put our Higher Power in charge of people, places and things while we work on ourselves. That is the idea of the Serenity Prayer: to accept the things we cannot change—which is other people, places and things—and to change the things we can, which is ourselves.

In order to change ourselves, we must recognize, admit and accept our assets as well as our liabilities. Self-acceptance means to see ourselves realistically—not better, not worse. We use our assets to build a better us, and we identify our liabilities in order to find what needs to be changed. As we progress in our recovery, we become empowered by the knowledge that when we are disturbed, acceptance is the answer. Disturbances are the stepping stones to freedom.

∽o∾

Affirmation: *Acceptance is the beginning of all my growth.*

Reflection: *How can I differentiate between things I can change and things I cannot change? Am I willing to work on the change list and place the others in my God box?*

Prayer Found in
Dr. Bob's Office

Humility is perpetual quietness of heart. It is to have no trouble. It is never to be fretted or vexed, irritable or sore; to wonder at nothing that is done to me, to feel nothing done against me. It is to be at rest when nobody praises me, and when I am blamed or despised, it is to have a blessed home in myself where I can go in and shut the door and kneel to my Father in secret and be at peace, as in a deep sea of calmness, when all about is seeming trouble.

Andrew Murray (1828–1917), South African religious leader

∽○∽

Affirmation: *I pray for a quiet heart.*

Reflection: *Am I at rest when blamed and despised?*

Two Alcoholics Meet

Instead of joining the merrymakers at the bar,
"Bill got the guidance to look at the
ministers' directory in the lobby."

Dr. Bob and the Good Oldtimers, p. 64

It is moving to think upon the actions of Bill Wilson, the cofounder of AA, on that monumental day when he turned away from the barroom to the telephone. However, Bill didn't make just one call that solved all his woes. He persisted through nine calls before he found the person who would play a role in AA history. On the ninth call he reached a woman who was to introduce him to Dr. Bob, who—with Bill—pioneered alcoholism recovery.

How many lives have been saved from Bill's decision to make a call?

Each day we have two options: one is to eat, the other is to grow! When we face our challenges, we can eat over them or grow through them. Recovery shows us the way to make the healthy choice. The telephone is still our lifeline, even if it takes nine tries to find help.

꙰

Affirmation: *I make three recovery phone calls every day.*

Reflection: *Am I willing to persist in my recovery or do I cave in after a few tries to reach out?*

The Powerful Here and Now

We learn to live one day at a time. The day that we focus on is this one, this moment in time. Just as ships are kept afloat by airtight compartments, living in "daytight" compartments will help keep us afloat in the sea of life.

In early recovery we learn about this slogan by applying it to staying abstinent—one day at a time. Quitting forever would be too big a feat. We don't want to think about never eating binge food again. To stay away from one bite, for one day, is far more achievable.

What we cannot think about doing for a lifetime, we can do for a day. This approach applies not only to addictive eating but to other life situations. We can break life down into manageable portions. By keeping our minds in the here and now, we can focus on what needs to be done and what can be achieved in the moment.

Sometimes we think that we have to get ready for next week or next month. Of course, we have to plan ahead; we plan today and live today. What we want to avoid is living in the future. No one can handle that. Living in the future produces fear. Living in the past creates guilt. Living in the now is manageable. The real power is in this moment.

❧

Affirmation: *I keep my mind before my nose—in the moment.*

Reflection: *Does my preoccupation with the past or the future disrupt my efficiency in the moment?*

ABCs of Food Management

Absolutely eliminate all trigger foods.

Balance carbohydrate with protein.

Cook without added fat, and get rid of high animal fat foods.

Diets don't work. Diet mentality doesn't work either!

Eliminate all trigger foods 100 percent.

Fresh and frozen foods are the best options.

Get support by attending meetings and food groups.

Hydration is crucial to recovery. Water hydrates; coffee and tea dehydrate.

Iodized salt often contains sugar. Check the ingredients.

Juiced fruit is not on the food plan, neither are dried fruit, bananas, grapes, cherries and mangos.

Keep exercise to about forty-five minutes. The food plan supports that level of exercise.

Label reading is crucial to recovery.

Meat, fish, poultry and eggs are high-protein foods that are very friendly to our brain chemistry. Limit pork, beef, lamb to three times per week.

Never use cooking spray with alcohol.

Order in restaurants by giving clear directions.

Plan, report, commit your food and then let go.

Quinoa is a terrific grain. Try it! Always buy whole, not white grains (but not wheat, spelt, triticale or kamut, which are forms of wheat).

Rice cakes and puffed cereals are refined carbohydrates. We don't eat them nor do we eat other puffed, popped or instant or quick grains.

Sugar wears many disguises. Be careful!

Travel with cups, scales and measuring spoons. In this way we manage volume.

Use a multivitamin. Good nutrition supports recovery.

Variety is important to avoid boredom, addictive foods and allergies.

When in doubt, leave it out. Only use foods with identifiable ingredients.

Extra food leads to volume binges. It is a sign of self-will.

Yogurt is great, but watch for tricky ingredients such as food starch.

Zero sugar, flour, wheat, plus all the other addictive substances. Watch your toothpaste and your medications too.

Let Us Write and Reflect
on the Past Week

✥

Did I attend an adequate number of meetings?

Did I exercise too little or too much?

Did I take a Tenth Step inventory on a daily basis?

Was I accountable and honest about my food planning and implementation?

What steps did I practice?

Was I resentful, angry, selfish, dishonest or fearful?

Was I generous, kind, tolerant, patient or useful?

Were my actions, words or communications unloving or unkind?

Do I need to ask for or grant forgiveness for my actions or attitudes this week?

Was my level of hydration adequate?

Did I practice sound nutrition, including vitamins and high-quality foods?

Have I kept something to myself that should be discussed with my sponsor, advisor or therapist?

What areas of my life need improvement?

What service did I perform to help another or my group?

What was my major character flaw this week?

What was my most admirable trait this week?

Did I practice restraint of tongue and pen?

Did I rationalize any destructive behavior?

What are the corrective actions that need to be taken based on this week's inventory? Do I owe any amends?

Attainable Affirmations:
God Revealed

An affirmation is a seed: Plant it, attend to it daily, give it time to sprout and grow. Then watch for the bloom.

∽∽∽

I choose to make life positive.
I take time to notice the good things I receive.
In my world, I enjoy harmony, good health and prosperity.

I am blessed.

Today's Stress Buster:
Get Up Earlier

Set the alarm fifteen minutes earlier to ensure that you have time for breakfast. If you must eat on the run, have breakfast breads ready in the freezer. To make them, mix together ¹/₂ cup oat bran, ¹/₂ cup egg whites, 6 ounces of fruit, and ¹/₃ cup powdered milk, add sweetener and cinnamon, if you wish, and bake at 350 degrees for about a half hour or until a toothpick comes out clean.

There but for the Grace of God Go I

We need to keep our memories green in order to maintain an attitude of gratitude. We may be inclined to recall the good times of parties and holidays and forget about the misery, shame and sick feelings of the disease.

When we get into recovery and things begin to get better, pride and ego may return. Working with a new person brings back memories of the days of early recovery when the disease had beaten us. We have a reminder that our present happiness is a gift from God.

We need to remember with gratitude that when we were miserable and full of fear, we were helped by those who put their faith in a Greater Power. Our sponsors and the members of our groups reached out and gave the hand of help to us.

In my first months of recovery I was told, "You can't keep it unless you give it away!" That is one of the paradoxes of recovery: Giving is keeping.

∽o∾

Affirmation: I keep my recovery by sharing it.

Reflection: How often do I reach out to a newer person by phone or Internet and at a meeting?

Meetings Are a Checkup from the Neck Up

Aren't meetings wonderful? We long for the fellowship that fills those rooms. Going to meetings with a friend, or meeting one there, is a special feeling. Frequently we even linger on for the meeting after the meeting.

Often we hear someone say they always feel better after the meeting than when they arrived. No wonder the meeting place is our "recovery schoolroom." Our teachers are wise and recovering folks. We go there to learn our lessons!

God speaks to us through the members of our fellowships. Others' stories enlighten, enliven and inspire us.

If we were to make a long list of the things we do to enhance our recovery, meetings would surely appear there. That's why we keep coming back. Meeting makers make it!

∽o∾

Affirmation: I cherish my meetings.

Reflection: Do I maintain an attitude of gratitude for my meetings? Have I supported meetings so that they will survive and flourish?

The List

We keep at hand an amends list from our Eighth Step of those people we had harmed, as identified in our Fourth Step and disclosed in our Fifth Step. Until amends are made, our spiritual progress will be blocked.

The question for today is, "Does our own name appear on this list?" From time to time, we hear at meetings that we were hurt the most and that our own names should top the list. Because we are the recipients of all of the benefits of our step work, we are not the focus of Step Eight.

After an honest assessment of harms done to others, we examine our willingness to make amends to them all. Discipline is the healing force of this step. Correcting the damage of our past recklessness takes courage, honesty, forthrightness, willingness and conviction to go forward.

෴

Affirmation: I am willing to make amends to those people I have harmed.

Reflection: Have I resisted making amends owed to particular people because of embarrassment, resentment or fear? How might I become willing to make amends to these people?

Bless Them, Bless Me

I must remind myself constantly that
I can never know any other person's motives and
conditioning. I must, for my own sake,
accept them as they are.

One Day at a Time in Al-Anon, p. 120

For those I hold in unforgiveness I pray
    to drop judgments and expectations
    to understand their pain and fear
    to pray for grace to pour upon them
    to love and accept them just the way they are today
    to recognize my defects
    to correct my ways
    to pray for grace to pour upon me
    to love and accept myself just the way I am today.

∽∘∾

Affirmation: I practice forgiveness for myself and others.

Reflection: Do I see myself and others in the light of understanding, love and compassion?

Let Us Write and Reflect
on the Past Week

∽∘∾

Did I attend an adequate number of meetings?

Did I exercise too little or too much?

Did I take a Tenth Step inventory on a daily basis?

Was I accountable and honest about my food planning and implementation?

What steps did I practice?

Was I resentful, angry, selfish, dishonest or fearful?

Was I generous, kind, tolerant, patient or useful?

Were my actions, words or communications unloving or unkind?

Do I need to ask for or grant forgiveness for my actions or attitudes this week?

Was my level of hydration adequate?

Did I practice sound nutrition, including vitamins and high-quality foods?

Have I kept something to myself that should be discussed with my sponsor, advisor or therapist?

What areas of my life need improvement?

What service did I perform to help another or my group?

What was my major character flaw this week?

What was my most admirable trait this week?

Did I practice restraint of tongue and pen?

Did I rationalize any destructive behavior?

What are the corrective actions that need to be taken based on this week's inventory? Do I owe any amends?

Do . . . or Do Not.
There Is No "Try"

Trying is dying. Trying does not get the job done.

We use a technique in therapy when a group member uses the word "try," we ask them to try to tie their shoelace. Of course, the unsuspecting and cooperative person would bend right over and tie the lace. But that is not trying—that is doing.

"Trying" is a very weak word. We do not try to get to meetings, work our steps or manage our food. We *do* it. We may kid ourselves with this weak word, which is probably part of our denial and rationalization system. It isn't honest. "Well, I tried. . . ."

Let's stop trying and do it!

∽o∾

Affirmation: I am firm in my plans and intentions to recover and complete my recovery tasks.

Reflection: Have I used the word "try" to fool myself or someone else? Did I realize on some level that I was not sincere?

Wherever You Go, There You Are

Think about this story of a particular recovering woman. She went from meeting to meeting, looking for just the right one. Each meeting fell short, never quite coming up to her standards. She disliked this meeting for one reason and that meeting for another. The location was wrong, the time too early or late, the group members talked too much or too little.

Finally, she asked her sponsor how she could find a meeting that would meet her requirements. Her sponsor replied, "It's like you stepped in doggie dung in your meeting shoes. Then you go from meeting to meeting complaining about the smell!" Whatever our brand of dung, we can't run away from it, it travels with us.

What needs to change? Usually, more than our shoes. Recovery is learning to love where we are—learning to be present in the moment without judgment, expectations, blame or criticism.

∽o∾

Affirmation: *I experience the moment with acceptance and simplicity.*

Reflection: *Have I used complaints as excuses to avoid meetings?*

It's Not Old Behavior
If I'm Still Doing It

Recently a friend talked about her intolerance, saying, "I really need to work on being irritated by my husband's absent-mindedness. I have been less than kind in my tone of voice and attitude. It's insulting to him. Intolerance is one of the ugliest things about me. It's all about my fear of not being in control."

What a wonderful thing to be able to clearly identify our character defects. In recovery, in order to rebuild relationships, we are able to evaluate and correct destructive behaviors and attitudes.

Addiction keeps us stuck in behaviors that we learned in childhood. Abstinence gives us the opportunity to look at those behaviors that are causing pain for ourselves and others. The old way would have been to blame them and excuse ourselves. The recovery way is to identify our shortcomings and to humbly ask God to remove them.

こん

Affirmation: *I humbly ask God to remove my shortcomings.*

Reflection: *How does my intolerance show itself? When I am wrong, do I promptly admit it?*

No Offense Taken

*"You make yourself and others suffer just as much when
you take offense as when you give offense."*

Ken Keys, *Handbook to Higher Consciousness*

What we see is what we get! When we perceive someone as offensive, we create our own suffering. There is no problem until we say, "That guy offends me." It is at that moment that the problem begins. There are two things to do when this occurs. First, we ask ourselves, "What is it about this person that reminds me of myself?" Then we go about correcting our own shortcomings. This is the real work of recovery. This approach turns a negative situation into a full blown learning experience. We become victims of our expectations of others and victorious when we use our discomfort to learn and grow. Real peace comes when we change ourselves and accept others exactly as they are without demands or expectations.

∽∘∾

Affirmation: *Changes are easy when I look at me.*

Reflection: *Today I will list everything that irritates me; then I will look to see what needs to be corrected in my behavior and attitudes.*

The Twelve Steps are the spiritual principles that guide us in our personal recovery. The founders of AA came up with twelve principles—Traditions—that keep our groups intact. These Twelve Traditions are to the groups what the Twelve Steps are to the individual. They are suggested principles that ensure the survival and growth of the group. Hammered out on the anvil of experience, they were designed to guide our groups. Personal survival and survival of our program depend on understanding and implementing these principles. We need to develop a personal regard for the Twelve Traditions and an awareness of our role in preserving the unity of our Twelve Step program. In recovery, we become practitioners of the Twelve Steps *and* the Twelve Traditions.

TRADITION EIGHT

"Our fellowship should remain forever nonprofessional,
but our service centers may employ special workers."

For those who need professional services, credentialed therapists who specialize in eating disorders are available. These services occur outside the boundaries of the Twelve Step program. Recovering professionals in the field of eating disorders must differentiate between which hat is worn: professional or personal.

Operating within the Twelve Step boundaries, we find one food addict freely sharing with another. Our contacts with other food addicts are never on a paid or professional basis. Occasionally the services of paid workers who perform tasks that volunteers cannot consistently cover are required. Intergroup secretarial work would be one example of such a paid position. On a personal level, we never seek a financial reward for our contributions to our fellowship. We give it away in order to keep it.

∽∾

Affirmation: *I freely share with others in recovery without thought of compensation.*
Reflection: *Do I generously share with other food addicts?*

Willingness

Willingness is readiness to take action or make a choice. It moves us toward decision making. When we are willing, we are open and receptive to new ideas; we are teachable!

With recovery comes learning, growth and change. The goal in abstinence is to change into someone new and whole.

Uncertainty, pride and fear are blocks to willingness. We know what binge food does for us. Even though it tears our lives apart we stick with it, sometimes even hoping that someday we will achieve better results without the ugly consequences. We are unwilling to let go of food until we find something that is more reliable or until our lives become unbearable. At that point, we become willing to pursue a new way of life in recovery.

෬

Affirmation: I am willing to grow and change because I have tried it and I like it.

Reflection: In what area of my recovery do I need to become more willing to change? I will address this unwillingness with my sponsor.

Let Us Write and Reflect
on the Past Week

Did I attend an adequate number of meetings?

Did I exercise too little or too much?

Did I take a Tenth Step inventory on a daily basis?

Was I accountable and honest about my food planning and implementation?

What steps did I practice?

Was I resentful, angry, selfish, dishonest or fearful?

Was I generous, kind, tolerant, patient or useful?

Were my actions, words or communications unloving or unkind?

Do I need to ask for or grant forgiveness for my actions or attitudes this week?

Was my level of hydration adequate?

Did I practice sound nutrition, including vitamins and high-quality foods?

Have I kept something to myself that should be discussed with my sponsor, advisor or therapist?

What areas of my life need improvement?

What service did I perform to help another or my group?

What was my major character flaw this week?

What was my most admirable trait this week?

Did I practice restraint of tongue and pen?

Did I rationalize any destructive behavior?

What are the corrective actions that need to be taken based on this week's inventory? Do I owe any amends?

A Win/Win

Occasionally, a situation is so win/win that it just announces itself to us. Those are the times we yell out, "Hey, that worked out just great for everybody." At other times, we have to work for a mutually satisfactory outcome. The work is worth the effort because when one person loses, everybody loses.

We cannot build a good outcome on another person's loss. Instead of putting up our dukes and fighting it out to the bitter end, the win/win players work together to identify individual needs and differences; to be adaptable to others' solutions; to communicate cooperatively; and to attack problems, not people. In that way, the best solution for everyone is found!

∽∘∾

Affirmation: *When you win, I win too!*

Reflection: *Am I a team player who applies win/win principles?*

When You Realize You've Made a Mistake, Quickly Correct It

We continue to take personal inventory and when we are wrong, we promptly admit it—and then correct that wrong. That's called keeping our side of the street clean.

What other folks do really doesn't matter. Our job is to keep ourselves in fit spiritual condition. The risk of relapse is too great to ignore these principles.

The practice of inventory keeps problems from festering. We can quickly identify and squelch the development of destructive patterns, get sponsor feedback, be accountable for our actions. By facing our personal wrongs instead of anyone else's errors, we put the focus where it belongs, on the person we can change: ourselves.

಼ംം

Affirmation: *I identify and correct problems at the first sign of trouble.*

Reflection: *Do I practice the use of a daily inventory in order to prevent destructive patterns from developing?*

A Five-Point Plan

A friend in strong recovery relates her plan when things go wrong:

1. I start my day over and do not slip into fear, remorse or self-loathing because I am exhibiting this behavior.
2. I acknowledge that I am at Step Six with this behavior, that I am powerless to change it and that I am entirely ready to have it removed.
3. I humbly ask my Higher Power to remove this judgmental, critical, blaming shortcoming of mine by saying the Seventh Step Prayer: *My Creator, I am willing that You should have all of me, good and bad. I pray that You now remove from me every single defect of character which stands in the way of my usefulness to You and my fellows. Grant me strength, as I go out from here to do Your bidding.*
4. I make amends each time I slip into this behavior as soon as it happens.
5. This evening at home, I will sit down quietly and write about my responsibility in these matters so that I will get a clearer understanding of what is going on with me.

∽∽∽

Affirmation: *I am responsible for my behavior.*

Reflection: *Am I willing to identify and ask God to remove my defects of character that stand in the way of my usefulness?*

Joy

*The future, higher evolution will belong to
those who live in joy, who share joy
and who spread joy.*

Torkom Saraydarian

Addiction keeps us in a state of numbness and depression. Each recovery day gives us the option to live a life of joy.

Did you ever notice how much joy there is around recovering people? Yes, there are lots of smiles and laughs in those joy-filled meeting rooms. That's because recovery is the pathway to joy. It opens up the possibility—actually the probability—of fun and laughter, joy and peace.

My sponsor told me, "We are in a program of recovery and a program of discovery!" Joy is one of those discoveries. Joy is the energy of the love expressed by one food addict for another. My friend suggests making a joy list: "That's a list of things that don't cost a lot of money but bring you joy."

∽o∾

Affirmation: I keep a list of things that bring me joy.

Reflection: Today, let's turn our minds to thoughts of joy by making a joy list.

Let Us Write and Reflect on
the Following Question

∽o∾

What are all the things I like about myself?

Don't Believe Everything You Think

Addiction keeps us trapped in our childhood belief system. We never grow up because we eat instead of dealing with life on life's terms. Maturity demands that we problem solve and learn to cope with the challenges of life. That cannot happen when we "eat over" our problems.

When we put down our numbing drug—food—we are defenseless! We never learned coping skills or problem solving, and the feelings come flooding up. Our job in recovery is to deal with our emotions, one at a time. Recovery requires us to grow emotionally, and the program shows us how.

What we are really dealing with is the thought that produces the feelings. When we change the thought, the feeling follows.

So here is the way it goes: The feeling comes up, acting like a messenger knocking on our door. It says, "Pay attention, there is work to be done!" We identify the feeling, then the thought that produced it. Also, an added dimension is to figure out the old belief (usually from childhood) that spawned the thought. We ask ourselves, *Is this thought helpful?* If it isn't, we change it to one that is beneficial.

When we change the thought, we dispel the painful feeling. We can get our sponsors to help us with this, talk about it at meetings, make phone calls to healthy recovery buddies or learn coping skills in therapy.

❧

Affirmation: *I identify my thoughts and feelings, change my thoughts, and enjoy peace.*

Reflection: *Do I cling to negative thinking that creates painful feelings? Am I willing to examine these thoughts in order to enjoy pleasant emotions?*

Let Us Write and Reflect
on the Past Week

ᔥᘏᔥ

Did I attend an adequate number of meetings?

Did I exercise too little or too much?

Did I take a Tenth Step inventory on a daily basis?

Was I accountable and honest about my food planning and implementation?

What steps did I practice?

Was I resentful, angry, selfish, dishonest or fearful?

Was I generous, kind, tolerant, patient or useful?

Were my actions, words or communications unloving or unkind?

Do I need to ask for or grant forgiveness for my actions or attitudes this week?

Was my level of hydration adequate?

Did I practice sound nutrition, including vitamins and high quality foods?

Have I kept something to myself that should be discussed with my sponsor, advisor or therapist?

What areas of my life need improvement?

What service did I perform to help another or my group?

What was my major character flaw this week?

What was my most admirable trait this week?

Did I practice restraint of tongue and pen?

Did I rationalize any destructive behavior?

What are the corrective actions that need to be taken based on this week's inventory? Do I owe any amends?

Let Us Write and Reflect on
the Following Idea

ベ〜

Clearly, if we are to live free of the bondage of compulsive eating, we must abstain from all foods and eating behaviors which cause us problems. . . . Many of us believed that our lives would be manageable if only others around us would do as we wanted.

Twelve Steps and Twelve Traditions of Overeaters Anonymous, p. 2-4

_____

_____

_____

_____

_____

_____

_____

_____

_____

_____

_____

_____

Retaliation

When we plan to get even with someone, the hurt continues. Releasing our anger when we are hurting is really hard. Processing it makes us feel righteous and we want to hang on to it.

Our thoughts of hatred, retaliation and revenge are toxic. These thoughts and feelings can overwhelm us as we fantasize about ways to get even. Yet our spirits long to exist without judgment, criticism, blame and expectations.

So how do we return to peace? The pathway back to peace is to let go. We let go by accepting responsibility for our thoughts. We have the power to change them from revenge to acceptance. We find the way to accept the people we cannot change. We give up the idea of revenge in order to find peace within ourselves.

∽∘∽

Affirmation: I put down the club of revenge for serenity.

Reflection: Am I willing to visualize good things happening to my "enemies"?

Getting Rid of CRAP

Caffeine
Refined carbohydrates
Animal fats
Processed foods

In our life of recovery, we give up a lot of crap—not just the food but our unhappy lives as well. In order to determine which path to follow, we need to examine all of the consequences of the disease and the benefits of recovery. One essential part of this task is to keep our memory of the disease process current, recalling the downward path of destruction we followed in the pursuit of addictive foods. Equally important is to review the benefits of recovery.

∽∘∾

Affirmation: *My life is filled with good food, good health and happiness.*

Reflection: *Today I will write two lists: one that includes the consequences of the disease and the other outlining the benefits of recovery.*

scheduling

When we eat is just as important as *what* we eat. Regularly scheduled meals keep us in a biochemically sound condition. Slowly released complex carbohydrates moderated by protein, eaten every four to five hours, keep our metabolism level, appeal to our body and brain chemistry, and keep us emotionally stable.

∞∞

Affirmation: I schedule my meals carefully to get optimum benefit from my food plan.

Reflection: What are the consequences of badly scheduled meals? What are the benefits of regularly scheduled meals?

Take a Breath!

Our friend the massage therapist reminds us to stop and take a few deep breaths.

Do a few minutes of deep breathing by inhaling through the nose to a count of seven, holding the breath after the inhale for about four seconds and then exhaling through the nose for a count of seven. Inhaling and exhaling through the nose slows down the breathing process and helps us become aware of our breathing.

This exercise does wonders in reducing stress levels and energizing our bodies.

∽∾∾

Affirmation: *I breathe deeply, inhaling tranquility, exhaling discord.*

Reflection: *Today I will practice deep breathing as a healthy recovery tool.*

Today's Stress Buster:
Discover Yourself

All we really have to do is discover ourselves. We can never know anyone as well as we know ourselves. Let's not miss the opportunity.

We have so much to learn. As we find out about ourselves, we discover corrections and endorsements to be made. We correct the ineffective parts of us and endorse the effective ones.

Focusing on other people is a waste of time. We need to concentrate on ourselves; get in touch with our needs; try new things; have some fun.

Let Us Write and Reflect
on the Past Week

∽◌∾

Did I attend an adequate number of meetings?

Did I exercise too little or too much?

Did I take a Tenth Step inventory on a daily basis?

Was I accountable and honest about my food planning and implementation?

What steps did I practice?

Was I resentful, angry, selfish, dishonest or fearful?

Was I generous, kind, tolerant, patient or useful?

Were my actions, words or communications unloving or unkind?

Do I need to ask for or grant forgiveness for my actions or attitudes this week?

Was my level of hydration adequate?

Did I practice sound nutrition, including vitamins and high-quality foods?

Have I kept something to myself that should be discussed with my sponsor, advisor or therapist?

What areas of my life need improvement?

What service did I perform to help another or my group?

What was my major character flaw this week?

What was my most admirable trait this week?

Did I practice restraint of tongue and pen?

Did I rationalize any destructive behavior?

What are the corrective actions that need to be taken based on this week's inventory? Do I owe any amends?

Up the Down Escalator

Greetings and prayers for all who have returned from relapse. Coming back takes courage and persistence.

The greatest relapse prevention tool is the inventory. Of course we take character-building inventories, but our recovery behaviors need to be inventoried too. When we take an honest inventory every night and identify the weak places in our program, we have a good chance of avoiding relapse.

Here is a recovery program inventory:

Did I get to a meeting today? How many meetings this week?
What steps did I work on today?
Did I call my sponsor and make two other phone calls?
Did I develop and implement a food plan?
Did I exercise, read literature, take my vitamins, journal, make a gratitude list?
Did I pray and meditate?
What character defects do I need to address tonight?

After doing this inventory, we can add anything we need to personalize our checklist in order to determine if our program is strong enough to withstand this powerful addiction.

∾∘∾

Affirmation: *A program inventory keeps me on my toes.*

Reflection: *How often do I take an inventory to catch weaknesses in my recovery program?*

Recovery First!

Recovery, without exception, is the most important thing in our lives. We may think that our jobs, families or friends take precedence. Certainly these are all of the utmost importance. However, consider that if we do not recover, chances are we won't have quality relations on the job, in the family or with our friends. In all probability we will lose our health and even our lives too.

Active addiction is a way of death, not a way of life. A food addict who is active in the disease tells us:

> *My humor, my energy, my vitality, is compromised by the inner turmoil of my obsessive behavior with food. I do not rest or sleep well because of the constant craving and depressed state. I have a hard time working at this point. Mental acuity is greatly diminished by my tired, physically compromised state. My work reflects these problems, and I know that I am not functioning at my best when this disease is in control.*

When we put other things first, we severely hurt our potential to recover. What we put before recovery, we lose.

Once we become convinced that everything in life depends on our recovery, we improve our chances of getting abstinent and staying abstinent so that we can have the life of our dreams.

∾◦∾

Affirmation: *My recovery comes first.*

Reflection: *Do I live a program that prioritizes my recovery by including step work, phone calls, planning, prayer, meditation, inventory, reading, writing and meeting attendance?*

Choices

Until we realize we have choices we may think, *I can't binge* or that we'll never get to eat that certain food again. That is painful thinking—stinkin' thinkin'!

The truth is, we are allowed to eat that food; we can binge if we wish. If our arm still bends and we can get hand to mouth, we can choose to eat anything we want. However, when we *choose* to stay abstinent, a whole world of options opens up to us.

Years ago, a friend in recovery told about her first week on the food plan. It was early evening when she told her daughter, "Well, I guess I will go to bed." Her daughter exclaimed, "Mom, it is only seven o'clock!" She answered, "I know but I have eaten everything on my food plan for today and there is nothing left to do!"

When compulsive eating is out of the way, we are left wondering how to spend our time. That's the point when our choices really open up. We realize we can do more than go to bed. All that time spent on eating, cooking, trips to the stores and restaurants, and hiding can be spent creating a whole new life. It is our first chance to become the person we want to be.

❧

Affirmation: *I have a list of good choices for today.*

Reflection: *What kind of person do I want to be?*

Attainable Affirmations:
Happy Days

Affirmations are constructive and positive. Repeating them overcomes the negativity we were accustomed to in addiction.

❦

I am responsible for my happiness.
I have the power to release all resentments, hurts and
unhappy memories. I am free.

Thinking Well of Ourselves

During all those years we spiraled downward in the disease of food addiction, we felt terrible. We ate to feel better and always felt worse—living life in shame and fear. Often we hated ourselves and blamed everyone around us.

Coming into recovery and grasping a plan of abstinence, we start to feel better about ourselves. However, gaining self-esteem is progressive. Abstinence is the beginning. When feeling dissatisfied, we reminded ourselves, *I did my best today, I can't do better than my best!*

In our inventory steps, we identified negative patterns that were developed before we had a positive course of action. Self-searching casts a light on our negative side. Now, we have a chance to change and grow. The full spectrum of the program is needed to experience growth—more than the food plan, more than meetings. We need all Twelve Steps. As we do our best every day in recovery, we learn that self-esteem is the byproduct of our worthy actions.

‿o‿

Affirmation: My best is good enough.

Reflection: Do I endorse my worthwhile behaviors while correcting my negative traits?

Body, Emotions, Mind and Spirit

We talk about our bodies, minds, emotions and spirits as though they are all separate parts. They are not. They cannot be separated like a yolk from an egg white. We are really body-emotionsmindspirit.

Let's look at how the whole person is involved in our anger. Anger is an emotion, but anger is a mental, spiritual and physical phenomenon. The mind spawns the anger with a thought: *That SOB outta be shot!* Then the emotional component—rage—follows. Our bodies are flooded with hormones that alter brain and body chemistry, causing physical changes such as trepidation, sweating and feeling hot. Anger puts us in a dangerous place spiritually. It takes us out of love, our spiritual ideal, and puts us in a place of unforgiveness.

Anger is an enemy of the body/emotions/mind/spirit—the whole person.

When anger comes, remind yourself: "This is the enemy, this is the ultimate enemy, this is the true enemy." An external enemy may, the next day, become a good friend. But anger, this inner enemy, is always the enemy.

His Holiness the 14th Dalai Lama,
Harvard University, September 10, 1995

ॐ

Affirmation: *I am honest about my anger, and I find appropriate ways to resolve it.*

Reflection: *Today I will meditate on these words: Love and acceptance are spirited principles and I choose to live a spiritual way of life.*

Let Us Write and Reflect
on the Past Week

∽⚬∾

Did I attend an adequate number of meetings?

Did I exercise too little or too much?

Did I take a Tenth Step inventory on a daily basis?

Was I accountable and honest about my food planning and implementation?

What steps did I practice?

Was I resentful, angry, selfish, dishonest or fearful?

Was I generous, kind, tolerant, patient or useful?

Were my actions, words or communications unloving or unkind?

Do I need to ask for or grant forgiveness for my actions or attitudes this week?

Was my level of hydration adequate?

Did I practice sound nutrition, including vitamins and high-quality foods?

Have I kept something to myself that should be discussed with my sponsor, advisor or therapist?

What areas of my life need improvement?

What service did I perform to help another or my group?

What was my major character flaw this week?

What was my most admirable trait this week?

Did I practice restraint of tongue and pen?

Did I rationalize any destructive behavior?

What are the corrective actions that need to be taken based on this week's inventory? Do I owe any amends?

Without Forgiveness, There Is No Future

The world is full of sickness. If we react with resentment to every sick person we meet, we will experience a life of total toxicity and live in hell. When we respond with love, we live in heaven on Earth because we are practicing a spiritual way of life.

We are aligned with God when we say, "I love and accept others just the way they are today, because love and acceptance are spiritual principles and I choose to live a spiritual way of life."

In the world of the spirit,
There is no right or wrong
Good or bad
Could or should
Only love and acceptance.

❦

Affirmation: I view myself and others with understanding, love and compassion.

Reflection: How does my critical nature keep me from love and peace?

Regrets

Do you have regrets? The great thing about them is that once they are identified, we can do something about them right *now*.

One day I was lamenting that I hadn't planted a gardenia bush when I moved into my house. Then I realized, *Heck, I can go get one right now*. All it took was a trip to the gardenia bush store and a little information off the Internet on their care and feeding.

No more regretting the lack of gardenias in the yard. Not that lacking the little bush was much of a regret, but it represents the way we correct our past transgressions. We do it now!

Unacceptable behavior that fills us with remorse can be healed by making amends in the present. We set things straight for past behavior, neglect and abuse of friends and family, financial irresponsibility, dishonesty and other transgressions.

Step Nine says we make "direct amends to such people wherever possible, except when to do so would injure them or others." We are cautious not to do further harm when we make our apologies and correct our errors. Above all, we commit to change our behavior.

∽∽∽

Affirmation: I am capable of changing and growing.

Reflection: Have I continued to make amends by staying abstinent, correcting past behaviors, helping others and growing spiritually?

Assertiveness

Assertiveness, standing between passive and aggressive behaviors, is the best choice of the three. The aggressive person is loud and demanding; the passive person says nothing; the assertive one speaks gently but firmly. Assertiveness is an honest and rational way that we can stand up for our beliefs and needs.

Assertive behavior is important to our abstinence. If we are passive about our needs in restaurants, or with friends and family, we will never be able to keep our abstinence. If we are aggressive, demanding and angry, we will ruin mealtime for ourselves and those around us. Assertion wins the day when we decisively ask for what we need and firmly return food that is inappropriate for our plan.

We feel better about ourselves when we state our case clearly. Because folks can't read our minds when we say nothing and can't figure out our needs when we are shouting, assertion improves relationships, leading to greater self-esteem, diminished anger and better communication.

కాం

Affirmation: *I assertively express my needs in a moderate but firm tone of voice.*

Reflection: *Am I assertive, aggressive or passive? How can I become more assertive?*

A Spiritual Awakening

We came. We came to. We came to believe. That process of coming into the program, awakening and finding our Higher Power is very personal.

The Twelve Steps are intentionally vague and open to each member's personal characterization of God. We can define our own spirituality.

We come into recovery in many different states of religiosity or animosity toward organized religion. The good news of recovery is that we can formulate a spiritual way of life and a conception of a Greater Power that fits for us.

Some might say that we must believe in a certain idea of God or the beliefs described in this book or that book. Well, those ideas of God are someone's conception of God. No two people see God exactly the same way, even if they sit right next to each other in the same church. We all bring our own experiences, intellect, biases and backgrounds with us. Each of us must find our own way. Some of us will return to the traditional orthodox practices of our childhood; some of us will strike out in a whole new direction. Whatever way we go, when we begin to practice God consciousness, our lives take on a whole new meaning.

∎

Affirmation: *I am spiritually awake.*

Reflection: *How has my spiritual life changed as the result of practicing the Twelve Steps?*

Listening

As Wilson Mizner says, "A good listener is not only popular everywhere, but after a while he gets to know something." In recovery we are advised to learn to listen and listen to learn. We need to heed that advice, because we don't learn a thing while we are talking.

Meetings are a good place to practice our listening skills. Most of our time is spent listening to, and hearing, what others share. A definite block to good listening at meetings is rehearsal: planning what to say when it is our turn. A better way is to listen intently for one helpful idea to take away from the meeting that will enhance our recovery.

Telephone calls are an opportunity to hone our listening skills too. Sponsors and recovery buddies call to talk. Hearing what they have to say gives them the support they need.

In certain situations, all that is needed is a good listener—a sounding board. Because we don't have all the answers, listening can be a comfort to those who need to talk. I learned a lot from a young woman who had lost her husband. She needed to talk about him. That's all—just talk about him. No words of comfort could have been as effective as allowing her to remember him out loud.

∽o∾

Affirmation: I learn to listen and listen to learn.

Reflection: I will practice listening skills by maintaining eye contact, hearing what is said and reflecting back to the speaker a significant statement.

Lower Your Expectations

A friend related that she had told her spouse that day, "Stay away from me, I don't like making amends!" A fair warning, I would say. Another acquaintance told her husband, "Lower your expectations of me today," which was a rather gentle way of saying the same thing.

Difficult days and bad moods come and go, and they test our recovery. When suffering, warning those around us is conscientious and considerate. Why let our loved ones walk into a thunderstorm?

Bad moods can lead to conflict with the people near and dear to us. Communicating our distress can save us from the pain of conflict with family members and friends. They may want to run for the hills while we call our sponsor.

∽o∾

Affirmation: I communicate my feelings honestly.

Reflection: Am I willing to issue storm warnings when my moods are distressing?

Let Us Write and Reflect
on the Past Week

∾∾

Did I attend an adequate number of meetings?

Did I exercise too little or too much?

Did I take a Tenth Step inventory on a daily basis?

Was I accountable and honest about my food planning and implementation?

What steps did I practice?

Was I resentful, angry, selfish, dishonest or fearful?

Was I generous, kind, tolerant, patient or useful?

Were my actions, words or communications unloving or unkind?

Do I need to ask for or grant forgiveness for my actions or attitudes this week?

Was my level of hydration adequate?

Did I practice sound nutrition, including vitamins and high-quality foods?

Have I kept something to myself that should be discussed with my sponsor, advisor or therapist?

What areas of my life need improvement?

What service did I perform to help another or my group?

What was my major character flaw this week?

What was my most admirable trait this week?

Did I practice restraint of tongue and pen?

Did I rationalize any destructive behavior?

What are the corrective actions that need to be taken based on this week's inventory? Do I owe any amends?

The Twelve Steps are the spiritual principles that guide us in our personal recovery. The founders of AA came up with twelve principles—Traditions—that keep our groups intact. These Twelve Traditions are to the groups what the Twelve Steps are to the individual. They are suggested principles that ensure the survival and growth of the group. Hammered out on the anvil of experience, they were designed to guide our groups. Personal survival and survival of our program depend on understanding and implementing these principles. We need to develop a personal regard for the Twelve Traditions and an awareness of our role in preserving the unity of our Twelve Step program. In recovery, we become practitioners of the Twelve Steps *and* the Twelve Traditions.

TRADITION NINE

"Our fellowship, as such, ought never be organized,
but we may create service boards or committees
directly responsible to those they serve."

The less organization the better! However, from time to time, committees are required to accomplish special projects such as literature development, conferences and other special events. These committees disband when the undertaking has been completed. Our groups may elect a secretary, treasurer, intergroup representative, literature person and someone responsible for the meeting place on a rotating basis. These services are much needed.

While these activities are very important to the fellowship, the basic work of Step Twelve is voluntary, individual and spontaneous— one addict carrying the message to another. On a personal level, we accept and carry out the jobs we perform for the fellowship with patience, humility and honesty.

∽◦∾

Affirmation: I bless the fellowship and I am blessed.
Reflection: How can I keep my ego out of the jobs I am assigned in the fellowship?

Into Action

Putting off something you hate to do? When disagreeable chores nag at us, we can save ourselves a lot of suffering by taking care of them as soon as possible. The longer we put it off, the more enormous it looks. When we roll up our sleeves and get to it, we can breathe a sigh of relief when the job is done.

∾

Affirmation: I do my chores with enthusiasm and good humor.

Reflection: Today I will tackle two jobs I have been putting off.

Surrender Goes On and On

Surrender begins when we hit bottom—when the pain of addiction becomes intolerable. Crying out for help is the beginning of an act of surrender that continues through all the years of our recovery.

Understanding comes from good information. Complete surrender depends on a clear grasp of the fact that we are powerless over our food addiction, which will grow progressively worse when we ingest trigger foods. We have then surrendered to the *fact* of our addiction. *"Surrender as much of yourself as you understand to as much of God as you understand,"* advised Sam Shoemaker. Aren't we always in some process of discovering more about ourselves and more about God, too? As our awakening and enlightenment increases, we are able to let go of more of our lives and wills to a Power we are learning to trust.

✧

Affirmation: *I keep surrendering what I don't need to God, whom I do need.*

Reflection: *Do I see surrender as a spiritual opportunity? Do I let go and let God manage for me?*

Beliefs

Beliefs are ideas learned during our lifetime that we start for-mulating in childhood. They are our attempts to make sense out of the world around us.

We each have our own set of beliefs. Some of them are rational and realistic, some are not. All of our beliefs are the parents of our thoughts. Rational beliefs create rational thoughts, while irrational beliefs create irrational ideas. Whether rational or irrational, we consider them all to be true. Without examination, we live and die with the ones that limit us as well as the ones that nourish us.

One method of self-examination is to challenge our thoughts by asking, *Is this thought helpful?* Any thought that creates pain is not helpful. After identifying unhelpful thoughts, we can change them. For instance, *Everybody is out to get me* is a thought that produces fear. That thought could be changed to *I have the support of many loving people,* which would produce feelings of security. By chang-ing thoughts, our limiting beliefs are challenged and changed too.

∽o∾

Affirmation: I identify, challenge and change unhelpful thoughts.

Reflection: How do my thoughts influence my emotions? In what way can I change my thoughts to create positive moods?

The Generosity Game

Although I have never had a secret pal, the concept is so *spiritual*. Doing a nice thing without getting caught—expressing love without any thought of return—is truly love without a price tag. Remember the "random acts of kindness" trend that promoted selfless acts? The whole idea was to spread kindness. What a bright spot in the day for both the receiver and the giver!

∽○∽

Affirmation: I love you just the way you are today!

Reflection: Today I will secretly surprise someone with a small reminder of how much they are loved.

I Am Really Disappointed!

Handling disappointment well is a sign of maturity. Disappointment usually means we didn't get something we wanted, resulting in feelings of discouragement, hurt or anger. When we lose the object of our desire, we don't want to lose the lesson too. When facing a disappointment, we can look at what can be learned from the situation:

Humility: It isn't realistic to expect to get our way every time.
Acceptance: It wasn't meant to be.
Perseverance: Keep on doing.
Flexibility: Time to change plans.
Perspective: Some losses make the wins sweeter.
Optimism: Start looking for something better.

∽∘∾

Affirmation: I always learn something from my disappointments.

Reflection: How might I turn a disappointment into a victory?

Let Us Write and Reflect
on the Past Week

∽◦∾

Did I attend an adequate number of meetings?

Did I exercise too little or too much?

Did I take a Tenth Step inventory on a daily basis?

Was I accountable and honest about my food planning and implementation?

What steps did I practice?

Was I resentful, angry, selfish, dishonest or fearful?

Was I generous, kind, tolerant, patient or useful?

Were my actions, words or communications unloving or unkind?

Do I need to ask for or grant forgiveness for my actions or attitudes this week?

Was my level of hydration adequate?

Did I practice sound nutrition, including vitamins and high-quality foods?

Have I kept something to myself that should be discussed with my sponsor, advisor or therapist?

What areas of my life need improvement?

What service did I perform to help another or my group?

What was my major character flaw this week?

What was my most admirable trait this week?

Did I practice restraint of tongue and pen?

Did I rationalize any destructive behavior?

What are the corrective actions that need to be taken based on this week's inventory? Do I owe any amends?

Let Us Write and Reflect on
the Following Question

၆၈

What negative and limiting thoughts are holding me back?

_____

_____

_____

_____

_____

_____

_____

_____

_____

_____

_____

_____

_____

_____

_____

_____

_____

Danette's Prayer

Thank you for the gift of beautiful abstinence. Thank you for the gifts of those who guide me, inspire me and teach me. Thank you for knowing what I do not know and leading me in the direction you want me to go. Thank you for loving me unconditionally and doing for me what I cannot do for myself. My life and will are yours. I trust that you know better than I what is best for me. Thank you for another glorious day to give and receive all that life has to offer.

∾⚬∾

Affirmation: *I gratefully let go and let God.*

Reflection: *Have I placed my life and my will in God's care today?*

"Volume" Is an Addictive Substance

Beware of eating volume. It will trigger active addiction.

A friend shared, "It is so clear to me—having put down sugar, flour, wheat and other binge foods—that my number-one addiction continues to be volume." Recognizing and surrendering to this fact underscore the importance of weighed and measured food, eating nothing more and nothing less than the food plan stipulates.

We cannot manipulate the food plan and win.

❧

Affirmation: My food plan is my best plan.

Reflection: Do I weigh and measure all my portions accurately, adding or subtracting nothing?

Let Us Write and Reflect on
the Following Idea

∽◦∾

Honesty, open-mindedness and willingness to change are all new attitudes that help us to admit our faults and to ask for help. We are no longer compelled to act against our true nature and to do things that we don't really want to do.

Narcotics Anonymous, p. 86

_____

_____

_____

_____

_____

_____

_____

_____

_____

_____

_____

_____

Consistency

If we don't have a consistent program, we don't have a program. Why? Because the day we neglect our recovery tasks, we won't get that day's reprieve from the disease. On those neglectful days, the door may open a bit or open completely, but the door will always open to the disease when we are casual about our recovery. What's more, we cannot predict how much disease will walk in the open door.

A friend shares, "I had a session with my therapist yesterday during which I came to understand that my stumbling blocks are inconsistency and casualness regarding my abstinence." One who has a consistent program knows that, "I will do today what worked for me yesterday and I can count on it to work again tomorrow."

⋄∘⋄

Affirmation: *I maintain a careful, thoughtful approach to recovery.*

Reflection: *Do I appreciate how consistency and inconsistency affect my recovery outcomes? What are some specific examples of my casual approach to recovery? What are the consequences that result from a casual approach?*

Don't Hurry

You are going to live forever—somewhere.
In fact, you are in eternity now; so why rush?

Emmet Fox

Emmet Fox's reminder to slow the pace of our everyday rushing about is instructive. We can either hurtle through eternity or slow down to a peaceful pace in order to enjoy the journey.

Remember the hare? Despite his rapid pace, he lost the race. The turtle moved slowly on his way, and because of that, he won the day!

∽o∽

Affirmation: *I inhale peace and exhale tension.*

Reflection: *Do I take time to slow my pace, quiet my mind and calm my jangled nerves?*

Let Us Write and Reflect
on the Past Week

～∘～

Did I attend an adequate number of meetings?

Did I exercise too little or too much?

Did I take a Tenth Step inventory on a daily basis?

Was I accountable and honest about my food planning and implementation?

What steps did I practice?

Was I resentful, angry, selfish, dishonest or fearful?

Was I generous, kind, tolerant, patient or useful?

Were my actions, words or communications unloving or unkind?

Do I need to ask for or grant forgiveness for my actions or attitudes this week?

Was my level of hydration adequate?

Did I practice sound nutrition, including vitamins and high-quality foods?

Have I kept something to myself that should be discussed with my sponsor, advisor or therapist?

What areas of my life need improvement?

What service did I perform to help another or my group?

What was my major character flaw this week?

What was my most admirable trait this week?

Did I practice restraint of tongue and pen?

Did I rationalize any destructive behavior?

What are the corrective actions that need to be taken based on this week's inventory? Do I owe any amends?

You Are Excused!

If you find an excuse to eat, don't use it! There are always excuses, but never a reason to eat addictively.

Excuses are killers before and during recovery. We excuse ourselves from meetings, making phone calls, weighing and measuring, and other crucial recovery responsibilities. If you find an excuse to slack off, don't use it. Because healthy behaviors require time, energy, effort and focus, excuses are made that perpetuate unhealthy practices.

A sure path back into the disease is the fatal habit of excuse making. The big risk is that we may be excused from recovery—permanently!

∽∾∾

Affirmation: *I count my many reasons to stay abstinent.*

Reflection: *Have I examined the excuses I make that compromise my recovery program? Do I watch for subtle excuses that undermine my resolve?*

Changing Routines

We need to guard against two kinds of routines. First are those routines that keep us in the disease—barriers to recovery. Second are those routines that lead us back into the disease—relapse traps.

Look at those things that trigger thoughts of eating: certain places, people, times of day and activities that are closely tied to addictive eating and drinking. If our route to work causes us to pass by the addictive breakfast-food place, drive another way. Instead of visiting relatives who serve dangerous foods, we invite them to our home where safe food is prepared. Watching television may trigger thoughts of binge foods. Turn it off!

We can read recovery literature instead, or make a phone call or write an evening inventory. Meeting the challenges and finding alternatives to the old way of doing things create a brand-new, exciting, healthy way of life.

∽∘∾

Affirmation: I will replace old routines with creative healthy practices.

Reflection: What old practices jeopardize my recovery? What behaviors are warning signs of relapse?

Don't Mess Up an Amends
with an Excuse

Can you see how excuse making will wipe out an amends? Making direct amends recognizes that our disease and our behaviors have hurt others.

We need to stop our destructive patterns. We cannot face the consequences of our behavior and clean up our pasts by making excuses. No excuse is required, even though a reason existed. We were out of control because we are addicts. Others were hurt during the progression of our disease. Once we see that our unmanageable lives were the result of the addictive process, the addiction looks less appealing.

When we use substances, our behavior is unacceptable. We break our own rules of conduct. Amends, made without justification, are the way back into a manageable life.

∽o∾

Affirmation: Making amends builds my character and corrects my past.

Reflection: Am I making direct amends to the persons identified in my inventories whom I have harmed?

Loneliness

Addiction is a lonely disease. Most of us didn't like to gorge in public, so secret, private places were best for that.

Isolation is a consequence of the addictive lifestyle. Even when we were in a room full of people, we could isolate by lack of good communication. Most of our meaningful conversations were with ourselves. So how do we resolve those lonely feelings?

A friend used to say to his kids, "To have a friend, you must be a friend." We can take the lead. Our meeting rooms are a good place to start. Get a phone number and invite someone for lunch, a hike or a movie. The fringe benefit is that we gain recovery support during the activity. Coming out of isolation is the benefit and healing grace of abstinent recovery.

∞∞

Affirmation: *I am surrounded by loving friends.*

Reflection: *Why not ask a new friend to share some time with me?*

Attainable Affirmations:
Positively Positive

Affirmations pay off. Positive, affirming people attract other positive people. Our affirming thoughts are like boomerangs. What we put out there, we get back.

∽०∽

I am surrounded by positive people.
I am grateful for my relationships.

Today's Stress Buster:
Staying Connected

Using the telephone is a way to reach out during hard times—either to ask for help or to give help. A phone call is our way out of isolation, which is a major relapse issue.

Phone calls can be our meetings between meetings. An important part of a good recovery program is to call one's sponsor on a daily basis in order to make a food plan commitment. We can even use those phone cards that allow us to dial 800 and place a really inexpensive phone call when we are traveling or attending a telephone meeting.

A meeting is always as close as our telephone. Phones are definitely the way to stay connected!

Let Us Write and Reflect
on the Past Week

～∞～

Did I attend an adequate number of meetings?

Did I exercise too little or too much?

Did I take a Tenth Step inventory on a daily basis?

Was I accountable and honest about my food planning and implementation?

What steps did I practice?

Was I resentful, angry, selfish, dishonest or fearful?

Was I generous, kind, tolerant, patient or useful?

Were my actions, words or communications unloving or unkind?

Do I need to ask for or grant forgiveness for my actions or attitudes this week?

Was my level of hydration adequate?

Did I practice sound nutrition, including vitamins and high-quality foods?

Have I kept something to myself that should be discussed with my sponsor, advisor or therapist?

What areas of my life need improvement?

What service did I perform to help another or my group?

What was my major character flaw this week?

What was my most admirable trait this week?

Did I practice restraint of tongue and pen?

Did I rationalize any destructive behavior?

What are the corrective actions that need to be taken based on this week's inventory? Do I owe any amends?

Abstinence, Sweet Abstinence

Abstinence opens the door to all possibilities. Just as our drug closes doors, abstinence opens them.

Look at those promises! So much joy can be found in this "new freedom and new happiness." With abstinence, we emerge from isolation and alienation to find that we can be happy and free. Free from craving and compulsion, we no longer have to "eat over" every challenge in life. The fog has lifted, we become clearheaded. We come to realize that our past was the training ground where we followed the process of addiction into recovery.

Because we are abstinent, we become useful in meaningful ways, sharing good information about food addiction recovery. We have found the answer.

∾o∾

Affirmation: *Abstinence from triggers is the foundation of my good life.*

Reflection: *Do I value abstinence as the pathway to a better life for me?*

His Coat

My father told me a story about when he was a young man. In those years in the early 1900s, some men rode railroad boxcars from town to town. They were called tramps, and they would walk through town asking for handouts. My grandmother's house was marked. She was a "good woman" who gave food to these men.

One cold day a tramp came to my grandmother's door without a coat. After feeding him, she told my dad to give him his winter jacket. My dad handed him his second-best jacket. My grandmother said, "No, give him your new one."

సిం

Affirmation: I send thanks to my spiritual advisers for the lessons they taught.

Reflection: Do I give the best I have to those who need me?

Where Disturbance Starts—and Ends

Great power lies in the knowledge that all of our disturbances start within ourselves. With that knowledge, we find that we are no longer victims of what goes on outside us. We are in charge of what we think and say and do. We don't have to take personally the thoughts and actions of the rest of the world.

When we are disturbed, a spot-check inventory can identify the cause of our disturbances. Usually we will have to give up our judgments, dissatisfaction and expectations.

A friend shares,

My daily goal is to remain as undisturbed as possible. In fact, I choose to remain serene, for if I am disturbed, clearly something is wrong with me. And for this food addict, that "something" needs to be addressed with a spot-check inventory, surrender, forgiveness of myself and others, amends where appropriate and right action in order to get back into the stream of life.

According to the AA *Twelve Steps and Twelve Traditions,* "A spot-check inventory in the midst of disturbance can be of very great help in quieting stormy emotions."

∞∞

Affirmation: *I evaluate and correct disturbing thoughts and behaviors.*

Reflection: *Do I take charge of my serenity by making spot-check inventories when I am disturbed? Then do I follow with the appropriate actions?*

Shame, Blame or Freedom?

First comes a judgment. Then we criticize and blame.

Shame and finger-pointing blame started with Adam and Eve, and we are still at it. *He did it, she did it, the snake did it.* That's what gets us in trouble. We point the finger and forget that four more are pointing back at us.

The idea, "if you spot it, you've got it!" has a lot of truth. In other words, we only see the things in others that bothers us about ourselves.

We overlook our responsibility and focus on what someone else did. That action leaves us as helpless, hopeless and powerless victims of our own judgment. We can't change "them," so we are without recourse, until we learn to give up the judgment. We can do that through an honest inventory: *What is it about this person that reminds me of myself? What are some examples of my behavior that matches this person's behavior? Who can I change? How can I change? What do I need to do differently? Have I given up my judgment of the other person?*

When we practice forgiveness, we become the kind of people we wish everyone else would be.

∽○∾

Affirmation: I do forgiveness work for positive change.

Reflection: What do I see in others that bothers me? In what ways am I the same as those who disturb me?

Life Is a Cinch by the Inch and Hard by the Yard

Life is difficult when we take on too much work at one time. A friend shares, "Slow and steady is the best way to build a solid foundation for your program. I was overwhelmed when I first tried to do everything at once." In all areas of life, tackling what is in front of us right here and right now is the best approach.

Being overwhelmed is a state of mind. Narrowing things down to prioritics can eliminate so much pressure. When we are suffocating, we don't worry about getting the bills paid. Our main concern is our next breath. Spiritual suffocation works the same way. Our major spiritual issues will always come up for resolution. We need to watch for them and deal with them as they arise. They will present as disturbing emotions—loud and clear. Once we identify the feeling, we ask, "What is the spiritual solution to this situation?"

Remember the song, "Love Is the Answer"? Love and acceptance are usually the answer to spiritual unrest. When love replaces anger and fear, we return to a fit spiritual condition. Affirming love is good for us, creating a healthy environment for our bodies, minds and spirits.

∽∘∾

Affirmation: I create love in place of anger and fear.

Reflection: Do I live by this code: Love and acceptance are spiritual principles, and I choose to live a spiritual way of life?

An Affirmation for Affirmations

A friend shares, "Work is hectic right now, or maybe it just seems that way because of distorted perceptions. So, I'm making efforts to turn the negativity around. This is another first for me in abstinence.

"The phone seemed to be ringing off the hook. With each ring I felt my anger and resentment rise as I thought, *Leave me alone.* The resentments kept growing and I prayed, *God, this is ridiculous, the phone rang just as much last week and I'm sure I wasn't like this.* So I wrote an affirmation and stuck it to my phone. It said, 'Thank you God for these calls from our wonderful clients who make this rewarding job possible for me!' It's been stuck there for an hour now. The first half hour I thought, *Yeah, right!* But now it's starting to sink in and it is working! I love the tools I learned in recovery."

Affirmations really do work!

᠅

Affirmation: *My positive thoughts calm me.*

Reflection: *How about putting a sticky note with an affirming thought on something that has been annoying me? (This idea may not work for spouses or other moving objects.)*

Let Us Write and Reflect
on the Past Week

ᢧᢀᢧ

Did I attend an adequate number of meetings?

Did I exercise too little or too much?

Did I take a Tenth Step inventory on a daily basis?

Was I accountable and honest about my food planning and implementation?

What steps did I practice?

Was I resentful, angry, selfish, dishonest or fearful?

Was I generous, kind, tolerant, patient or useful?

Were my actions, words or communications unloving or unkind?

Do I need to ask for or grant forgiveness for my actions or attitudes this week?

Was my level of hydration adequate?

Did I practice sound nutrition, including vitamins and high-quality foods?

Have I kept something to myself that should be discussed with my sponsor, advisor or therapist?

What areas of my life need improvement?

What service did I perform to help another or my group?

What was my major character flaw this week?

What was my most admirable trait this week?

Did I practice restraint of tongue and pen?

Did I rationalize any destructive behavior?

What are the corrective actions that need to be taken based on this week's inventory? Do I owe any amends?

God, Help Me to Want
What I Have

The literature talks about being "restless, irritable and discontent" in recovery: RID. We definitely want to get RID of those discomforting feelings. They signal a "dry drunk," which is when we walk around abstinent but unhappy.

What are we unhappy about? Here is what we might hear ourselves saying:

I'm not thin enough.
I don't have any friends.
Nobody likes me.
This food plan is boring.
I can't live without a _____. (Fill in the blank.)
I can't stand another one of those meetings.
My sponsor infuriates me.

The prescription is to get to work. Reading, writing, meetings, a step assignment—in fact, any recovery action starts to pull us out of it. Speak to a newer member. Listen with empathy to their challenges. Pray to be "relieved of bondage of self." Rewrite all of the negative self-talk. Make a gratitude list.

∽∘∾

Affirmation: *I use my energy for positive growth.*

Reflection: *How will I use positive self-talk to defeat negative ideas today?*

I Am a Unique Child of God

I am who I am,
I know what I know,
I can do what I can do,
That's good enough.

∽∘∾

Affirmation: *I know I am enough to be my best.*

Reflection: *Do I accept myself just the way I am today?*

The Twelve Steps are the spiritual principles that guide us in our personal recovery. The founders of AA came up with twelve principles—Traditions—that keep our groups intact. These Twelve Traditions are to the groups what the Twelve Steps are to the individual. They are suggested principles that ensure the survival and growth of the group. Hammered out on the anvil of experience, they were designed to guide our groups. Personal survival and survival of our program depend on understanding and implementing these principles. We need to develop a personal regard for the Twelve Traditions and an awareness of our role in preserving the unity of our Twelve Step program. In recovery, we become practitioners of the Twelve Steps *and* the Twelve Traditions.

TRADITION TEN

"Our fellowship has no opinion on outside issues;
hence, our name ought never be drawn into public controversy."

On a daily basis, a glance at the newspaper reports death and destruction resulting from political and religious conflict. In order to maintain integrity and purpose, our fellowship does not get involved in such issues and controversy. Peacefully going about its primary business of relaying the message of recovery to the still-suffering food addict, our fellowships have learned to stay out of public controversy. On a personal level, we discourage and refrain from bringing outside issues to our group for discussion.

∾∾

Affirmation: My meeting place is a peaceful place to grow.

Reflection: To ensure a peaceful meeting environment, I will guard against discussing any controversial outside issues in the meeting room.

First Things First

I have a friend who told me he was always the first to say hello when he met someone. That he was gracious and well-liked is no surprise. His comment made me realize that I sometimes waited to be acknowledged.

I tried saying "Hi" first, and I liked it. What an enlightenment! It felt loving, open and kind-spirited.

Next I tried being the first to say "I love you" and "I'm sorry." No surprise: I learned to like myself!

∽∘∾

Affirmation: *I am the first to say "Hello" to those I meet along the way.*

Reflection: *What are the benefits of being open and friendly?*

Thanks for the Compliment!

Never interrupt when someone is paying you a compliment. Fending off compliments is a sign of low self-esteem or false humility. We might say things like, "Aw shucks, this old outfit," or "It was nothing." Rejecting a compliment suggests that the person giving it has poor taste or is insincere.

Ideally, when someone pays us a compliment, we avoid protesting or denying the truth of the statement. We can accept the compliment graciously and with thanks. It takes practice.

Accepting a compliment doesn't mean we are conceited. Rather, such behavior indicates we have a healthy self-image. Compliments are nice to hear, so why not accept them? We deserve all the nice things people say about us.

∽∾

Affirmation: *I acknowledge my accomplishments. I accept and enjoy compliments.*

Reflection: *When given a compliment, do I look at the person and say "thank you" with a smile?*

Read More Books and Watch Less TV

Television can be stressful. We think of it as relaxing, but much of what we see on television is violent, noisy, intrusive and time-consuming. TV can actually interfere with our recovery.

Binge eating in front of the TV has become a way of life, maybe even overriding meetings, phone calls and other recovery obligations. TV could be another of our addictions. In a *Scientific American* article the authors state, "Most of the criteria of substance dependence can apply to people who watch a lot of TV."

Here are variations of the four questions we ask to screen for addiction.

Have you ever felt the need to reduce your level of television consumption?

Have people ever annoyed you with their criticism of your television behaviors?

Have you ever felt guilty about time spent watching TV?

Have you ever used television to "feel better," or to avoid people and responsibilities?

When these questions point to a television problem, we may need to reevaluate our relationship with it.

∽₀∾

Affirmation: I use my time for my spiritual benefit.

Reflection: Is abstinence from TV difficult for me?

Let Us Write and Reflect
on the Past Week

∽◦∽

Did I attend an adequate number of meetings?

Did I exercise too little or too much?

Did I take a Tenth Step inventory on a daily basis?

Was I accountable and honest about my food planning and implementation?

What steps did I practice?

Was I resentful, angry, selfish, dishonest or fearful?

Was I generous, kind, tolerant, patient or useful?

Were my actions, words or communications unloving or unkind?

Do I need to ask for or grant forgiveness for my actions or attitudes this week?

Was my level of hydration adequate?

Did I practice sound nutrition, including vitamins and high-quality foods?

Have I kept something to myself that should be discussed with my sponsor, advisor or therapist?

What areas of my life need improvement?

What service did I perform to help another or my group?

What was my major character flaw this week?

What was my most admirable trait this week?

Did I practice restraint of tongue and pen?

Did I rationalize any destructive behavior?

What are the corrective actions that need to be taken based on this week's inventory? Do I owe any amends?

Identify, Don't Compare

We thought that no other person acted with food as we did: secret stashes, eating in hidden places, consuming mass amounts of personal binge foods. Then we joined a program and found people whose patterns may have been different.

Comparing is looking for a way out. Listing all the things we didn't do can lead us to conclude that we are not really "like them," so admitting addiction and surrendering in recovery must not be the answer.

Identifying represents an attitude of recovery. We go to meetings with an open mind, listening to the sharing to see if we can identify with it. We find that we were all very much the same. We had the same downward progression, negative consequences, feelings, character defects and attitudes. We learned our similarities by identifying, not comparing. Identifying keeps us close and safe with other food addicts.

∽∘∾

Affirmation: By identifying, not comparing, I learn more about myself.

Reflection: Do I make an effort to identify with the speaker at meetings?

Ego's Weight-Loss Program

When the ego stops eating the soul begins.

Bob Marks

Feeding our spirits while stuffing our faces doesn't work. Active addiction is an absolute block to spiritual growth.

Ego wants us to keep making worldly choices: food, drugs, sex, alcohol. Recovery demands we make spiritual choices. We either reach for God or for food. When we get abstinent, food thoughts will intrude. When we obsess about food, God alone can help us reject these thoughts. All we have to do is ask.

&ao&

Affirmation: *I feed my spirit so that there will be more God and less me.*

Reflection: *How is my ego interfering with my recovery right now?*

Let Us Write and Reflect on
the Following Question

∽o∾

What people or areas of my life need forgiveness and acceptance?

A Sound Foundation

Our abstinence from highly refined foods and all other mood-altering chemicals constitutes not only the beginning of recovery, but the absolute foundation of recovery from food addiction.

Abstinence is not *giving up* something; abstinence is *getting rid* of something. We get rid of unwholesome food, craving, obesity, mental anguish, guilt, fear, physical illnesses, irritability, lethargy, downward progression and any number of other addiction-related destructive consequences.

✎∘✎

Affirmation: I definitely choose abstinence with all its benefits.

Reflection: Do I practice abstinence by planning, weighing, measuring, reporting and implementing my clean food plan?

Let Us Write and Reflect on
the Following Idea

꒰ঌ০঩꒱

For those who believe, no proof is necessary. For those who don't believe, no proof is possible.

John and Lyn St. Clair Thomas, *Eyes of the Beholder*

Addiction:
Powerful, Progressive, Persistent

During any period of abstinence, our disease is off on the sidelines doing pushups. We have read and listened to enough stories to realize that long-term recovery does not provide a comfortable relapse. Relapse won't take us back to the early days of addiction.

While we are hard at work on our recovery, addictive disease progresses, growing more resilient. It beckons us back into its trap with ideas like these:

"You have been in recovery for a long time; surely you could eat just one bite."

"Why not go off the food plan today and right back on tomorrow?"

"Just a little bit will make you feel better—you can handle it."

"Everyone else is having some, and it isn't hurting them."

Addiction doesn't quit! That's why we can't become complacent. We must challenge those thoughts with recovery answers:

"Since I have been in recovery a long time, I will make it another day longer and abstain from that first bite!"

"If I go off the plan today, I cannot predict when, if ever, I will get back on it."

"I don't eat to feel better. Binge food always makes me feel worse."

"Even though everyone is eating refined and processed foods, I choose the high-quality, nutritious food on my plan."

∽∽

Affirmation: I accept invitations to recover. I refuse invitations to relapse.

Reflection: Do I keep my program current and challenge thoughts that invite me back into the disease?

Let Us Write and Reflect
on the Past Week

∽∘∾

Did I attend an adequate number of meetings?

Did I exercise too little or too much?

Did I take a Tenth Step inventory on a daily basis?

Was I accountable and honest about my food planning and implementation?

What steps did I practice?

Was I resentful, angry, selfish, dishonest or fearful?

Was I generous, kind, tolerant, patient or useful?

Were my actions, words or communications unloving or unkind?

Do I need to ask for or grant forgiveness for my actions or attitudes this week?

Was my level of hydration adequate?

Did I practice sound nutrition, including vitamins and high-quality foods?

Have I kept something to myself that should be discussed with my sponsor, advisor or therapist?

What areas of my life need improvement?

What service did I perform to help another or my group?

What was my major character flaw this week?

What was my most admirable trait this week?

Did I practice restraint of tongue and pen?

Did I rationalize any destructive behavior?

What are the corrective actions that need to be taken based on this week's inventory? Do I owe any amends?

Can't or Won't?

How we label something has an effect on how we experience it. Often we believe our own propaganda. When we say we "can't" do something, and we really mean "won't" do it, the word choice changes the experience. When we don't want to take responsibility for our acts or decisions, we say "can't," meaning "not able" or "incapable." What we really mean is, "I don't want to, I refuse, I won't do it, I am unwilling."

When we change "can't" stay abstinent to "won't" stay abstinent, or "can't" meditate to "won't" meditate, the whole picture changes.

Getting honest and changing from "can't" to "won't" gives us the insight and opportunity to pray for willingness.

∽◦∾

Affirmation: *I have the courage and strength to speak directly and honestly.*

Reflection: *Do I choose my words carefully in order to be honest?*

Imagine That!

What would a mature adult do in this situation? I love to ask myself questions like that. Imagine what an adult would do, then go ahead and do it the mature way.

Sometimes I ask myself, *What would a composed person do at a time like this?* I really admire composure. Something is so "together" about it. I like to display great composure.

Other times I might think, *What would a good-humored person do about this?* Then I think of a joking, lighthearted way to respond to a situation. All of these responses are so superior to the frantic, reactive, out-of-control, obsessive addict that resides within. So many choices, so little time!

∽o∾

Affirmation: I act, instead of reacting, by choosing appropriate responses.

Reflection: Can I use my imagination to choose mature responses to distressing circumstances?

The Twelve Steps: A Toolbox with a Wrench for Every Nut

"Everybody makes mistakes. Fools repeat them, the weak excuse them, only the wise admit and profit from them." That is what recovery is all about.

Finding and profiting from our errors gets pretty exciting, like detective work. We have to get past the denial and delusions of perfection, find the defects that cause our discomfort, then enjoy the lesson and the relief.

Admitting and learning from our mistakes is the work of the Twelve Steps. For corrective actions, we have the best kind of guidance in the inventory and amends steps, plus sponsors to help us. With these tools, we become the wise ones.

∽o∾

Affirmation: *I profit from my mistakes by using the steps to learn new lessons.*

Reflection: *Which step am I working on today?*

Kate's Relapse Prevention Ideas

I get on my knees every morning and ask God to keep me away from that first bite. At night, I get on my knees again and thank Him for helping me to stay away from that first bite.

Whenever I experience the phenomenon of craving or food obsessions, I look at my last twenty-four hours. Did any hidden sugar, flour, wheat, caffeine or alcohol creep into my food? Did I eat at a restaurant? Did I try a new brand of canned food? Have I been getting enough sleep?

I came close to relapse when my mental obsession with food was almost unbearable. This thinking came during a period when I had three consecutive nights of six hours of sleep or less. I called a recovering friend who helped me through it.

No Food Recovery meetings within thirty minutes of me focus on abstinence. Instead, I go to many AA meetings, online and telephone meetings where abstinence is the focus.

∽∘∾

Affirmation: *I am willing to go to any lengths to recover from food addiction.*

Reflection: *Do I keep my recovery program active, even when it is not convenient?*

More Relapse Prevention
Ideas from Kate

I took phone numbers of people from the loop in all time zones and call them. I joined the loop by going to *www.kaysheppard.com* and following directions.

I have a sponsor who is unconditionally abstinent on the food plan whom I call every morning.

I rotate my foods. In previous abstinence attempts, I would eat essentially the same thing every day. Rotation is great and I never get bored. I started experimenting with spices and abstinent foods I hadn't tried before. After over three years in and out of the program and the most hellacious relapse of my life, I finally realized that my disease was serious, waiting to kill me, and that my disease is a primary disease, not secondary to alcoholism. Once I realized that, doing whatever it took to get and stay abstinent was a lot easier.

∽◦∾

Affirmation: *I take my recovery seriously.*

Reflection: *How did I come to terms with the serious nature of the disease of food addiction?*

Self-Will Versus God's Will

Here is what we know about the use of will:

Self-will is deadly.
Self-will keeps us stuck in old self-defeating patterns.
Getting rid of self requires God's aid.
Our program is one of ego deflation at depth.
Losing self-will requires rigorous honesty.
Opportunities for change present themselves when we are ready.
We lose the unrewarding part of self—our defects of character.
Self-will returns without continued discipline.
Seeking God's will is the proper use of our will.

∽o∾

Affirmation: I welcome the loss of my will for the benefits of God's will.

Reflection: In what ways do I cooperate with God's plan for me?

Let Us Write and Reflect
on the Past Week

౼౽౴౾

Did I attend an adequate number of meetings?

Did I exercise too little or too much?

Did I take a Tenth Step inventory on a daily basis?

Was I accountable and honest about my food planning and implementation?

What steps did I practice?

Was I resentful, angry, selfish, dishonest or fearful?

Was I generous, kind, tolerant, patient or useful?

Were my actions, words or communications unloving or unkind?

Do I need to ask for or grant forgiveness for my actions or attitudes this week?

Was my level of hydration adequate?

Did I practice sound nutrition, including vitamins and high-quality foods?

Have I kept something to myself that should be discussed with my sponsor, advisor or therapist?

What areas of my life need improvement?

What service did I perform to help another or my group?

What was my major character flaw this week?

What was my most admirable trait this week?

Did I practice restraint of tongue and pen?

Did I rationalize any destructive behavior?

What are the corrective actions that need to be taken based on this week's inventory? Do I owe any amends?

Misfortune? Good Fortune? Who Knows?

A Chinese story tells of an old farmer who had an old horse for tilling his fields. One day the horse escaped into the hills. When all the farmer's neighbors sympathized with the old man over his misfortune, the farmer replied, "Misfortune? Good fortune? Who knows?"

A week later, the horse returned with a herd of wild horses from the hills, and this time the neighbors congratulated the farmer on his good fortune. His reply was, "Good fortune? Misfortune? Who knows?"

Then, when the farmer's son was attempting to tame one of the wild horses, he fell off its back and broke his leg. Everyone thought this very bad misfortune. Not the farmer, whose only reaction was, "Misfortune? Good fortune? Who knows?"

Some weeks later, the army marched into the village and conscripted every able-bodied youth they found there. When they saw the farmer's son with his broken leg, they let him off. Now was that good fortune? Misfortune? Who knows?

Then the horse disappeared. Now was that good fortune? Misfortune? Who knows?

Things are not as they appear. Who knows? So we thank God for all that comes our way, without judgment, without complaint. We wait to see, because nothing is as it seems. More will be revealed.

∽⌒∽

Affirmation: *I withhold judgment while waiting for more to be revealed.*

Reflection: *Do I label things that happen as either good or bad?*

Attainable Affirmations:
Compassion

Compassion is kindness in action, the way to help ourselves by helping others. What might the results be from one act of loving kindness? Try it and see.

∽○∽

I am a competent, compassionate, caring, capable person.
I see myself and others with understanding,
love and compassion.

God's Pumpkins

A woman was asked by a coworker, "What is it like to be a recovering food addict?" The coworker replied, "It is like being a pumpkin. God picks you from the patch, brings you in and washes all the dirt off of you. Then he cuts off the top and scoops out all the yucky stuff. He removes the seeds of doubt, hate, greed. Then He carves you a new smiling face and puts His light inside of you to shine for all the world to see."

∞

Affirmation: *My Higher Power lights up my life.*

Reflection: *Have I realized that God has done the work of my deliverance, I just need to cooperate?*

Gratitude Month

A friend says, "I am so filled with gratitude instead of stuffed with food. What a thankful concept for gratitude month."

In many ways, addiction is the disease of ingratitude. We never have enough. Not enough food, attention, affection, cooperation or material goods. We whine, manipulate, spend, beg, buy, steal, demand, and are never satisfied.

Recovery changes all that. Today and every day we can say, "Let the attitude be gratitude." Gratitude will bathe every cell of our being with peace and satisfaction.

∽○∾

Affirmation: I am filled with gratitude.

Reflection: How do I show my gratitude for all the gifts I have received?

Evaluate and Endorse

We evaluate our conduct against our own rules. With the help of our sponsor, we develop a checklist determining what constitutes our most effective recovery program. We then use the checklist for our evening inventory.

We correct behavior that is ineffective and endorse ourselves for behavior that works. We develop a realistic recovery plan comprising those elements we need to maintain physical abstinence as well as emotional and spiritual growth. Our recovery list might include recovery meetings, sponsor contacts, food management guidelines, telephone calls, recovery literature, prayer, service and our Twelve Step study program. We each add our own important "musts" to the list.

～∞～

Affirmation: I endorse myself for today's recovery efforts.

Reflection: Do I have a checklist of the recovery tasks I need to maintain physical, emotional, mental and spiritual recovery?

In or Around Program?

One of our members had surgery, so we took a meeting to her bedroom. She was in a recliner chair and we all formed a circle around her. During the course of our discussion, we talked about whether we were "in" the program or just "around" it.

I got into her bed and perched on the edge, saying, "This is what it is like being on the edge of the program and ready to fall off." Then I got securely into the middle of the bed. "This is what it is like being 'in' the program. It feels much more secure."

We have searched for the "quick fix," the easier, softer way. Nothing will take the place of a firm commitment to the daily practice of recovery tasks by getting right into the middle of things!

∽∘∾

Affirmation: I reap the rewards from my firm commitment to recovery tasks.

Reflection: Have I surrounded myself with the tools, people and situations that support my abstinent recovery?

Prayer and Meditation

Isn't the best prayer, "Help"? Two other good ones are, "Show me the way" and "Thank you."

One thing the program makes quite clear is that we "pray only for knowledge of His will for us." We stop giving directions and start taking them.

This move is a real about-face for an addict. The practice of meditation or "quiet sitting" is also a switch. To slow down and sit quietly in order to achieve spiritual growth, peace, relaxation and relief from stress is often a dramatic change for us. A "treasure trove" of ways to meditate is available. Finding the best way to pray and meditate is personal and exciting.

∽∘∾

Affirmation: I practice the presence of God by praying and meditating.

Reflection: Have I found a way to pray and meditate that works for me?

Let Us Write and Reflect
on the Past Week

∽o∾

Did I attend an adequate number of meetings?

Did I exercise too little or too much?

Did I take a Tenth Step inventory on a daily basis?

Was I accountable and honest about my food planning and implementation?

What steps did I practice?

Was I resentful, angry, selfish, dishonest or fearful?

Was I generous, kind, tolerant, patient or useful?

Were my actions, words or communications unloving or unkind?

Do I need to ask for or grant forgiveness for my actions or attitudes this week?

Was my level of hydration adequate?

Did I practice sound nutrition, including vitamins and high-quality foods?

Have I kept something to myself that should be discussed with my sponsor, advisor or therapist?

What areas of my life need improvement?

What service did I perform to help another or my group?

What was my major character flaw this week?

What was my most admirable trait this week?

Did I practice restraint of tongue and pen?

Did I rationalize any destructive behavior?

What are the corrective actions that need to be taken based on this week's inventory? Do I owe any amends?

We Don't Carry the Food Addict.
We Carry the Message

We carry the message, not the mess.

A sponsor doesn't keep someone abstinent, doesn't have all the answers and isn't anyone's savior. All a sponsor really can do is show by example and make suggestions.

A friend in the program used to say, "We aren't bankers handing out loans, or taxi drivers or counselors." Sponsors share their experience, strength and hope with those they sponsor. A good way to avoid sponsor burnout is to abstain from expectations. What does a good sponsor offer? Acceptance, support, good information, honesty and availability.

∽∽

Affirmation: We share our experience, strength and hope with each other.

Reflection: Do I understand the limitations and responsibilities of sponsorship?

Action Alleviates Anxiety

When anxious, "action" is the magic word. Many actions bring health and happiness into our lives.

Telephoning to give and get help
Exercising
Writing, including step study, journaling and forgiveness work
Going to meetings
Reading recovery literature
Planning, reporting, committing food

Above all, the actions taken in working the Twelve Steps are the most important actions we can take.

࿇

Affirmation: *Action is the magic word.*

Reflection: *What actions work for me to alleviate anxiety?*

What Is in There

"Who are you?" said the caterpillar.
This was not an encouraging opening for a conversation.
Alice replied rather shyly, "I—I hardly know,
Sir, just at present—at least I knew who I was when
I got up this morning, but I think I must have
changed several times since then."

Lewis Carroll, Alice in Wonderland,
from *Through the Looking Glass*

Doesn't it seem frightening to look within? Fearing that we would only find terrible things, we are surprised to find the beauty there.

My friend says she feels like she is peeling an onion as she discovers layers of truths about herself. Self-searching is uncommon for us, yet as we grow in the program we come to learn the safety of looking inside. The action is really more like mining for gold than peeling an onion. All of our riches are right there inside.

◦∽◦

Affirmation: Each time I look inside, I find hidden treasures.

Reflection: Has fear kept me from my search for self?

Today's Stress Buster:
Unclutter Your Life

Start to unclutter your life by getting two trash bags. Put twenty-seven items to give away in one of the bags. Put twenty-seven items to throw away in the other bag. Spend fifteen minutes a day doing this and the clutter will disappear.

Put your Clutter Project on your to-do list. Be sure to talk to your sponsor about the pain of letting go of all that "stuff."

The Twelve Steps are the spiritual principles that guide us in our personal recovery. The founders of AA came up with twelve principles—Traditions—that keep our groups intact. These Twelve Traditions are to the groups what the Twelve Steps are to the individual. They are suggested principles that ensure the survival and growth of the group. Hammered out on the anvil of experience, they were designed to guide our groups. Personal survival and survival of our program depend on understanding and implementing these principles. We need to develop a personal regard for the Twelve Traditions and an awareness of our role in preserving the unity of our Twelve Step program. In recovery, we become practitioners of the Twelve Steps *and* the Twelve Traditions.

TRADITION ELEVEN

"Our public relations policy is based on attraction rather than promotion; we need always maintain personal anonymity at the level of press, radio and films."

No pressure tactics, no marketing, no recruitment! Our public relations policy is one of attraction. No celebrities, recovering or not, are hired to promote the program at the level of press, radio, films, television or any other public media.

The Eleventh Tradition protects the fellowship. There is no need for self-recommendation; better to "let our friends recommend us."

For our fellowships, no promotion is necessary, because the fellowship offers an effective alternative to addictive disease. On a personal level, we guard against anonymity violations in the public media. When we use our names, we do not identify affiliation with any Twelve Step program. If we do discuss program membership, we decline to use our names and prohibit the publication of our image, thus preserving our anonymity.

Affirmation: Anonymity is a spiritual principle that I embrace.
Reflection: Do I accept personal responsibility in maintaining anonymity at the public level in order to keep our fellowship safe?

Let Us Write and Reflect
on the Past Week

⮌⮎

Did I attend an adequate number of meetings?

Did I exercise too little or too much?

Did I take a Tenth Step inventory on a daily basis?

Was I accountable and honest about my food planning and implementation?

What steps did I practice?

Was I resentful, angry, selfish, dishonest or fearful?

Was I generous, kind, tolerant, patient or useful?

Were my actions, words or communications unloving or unkind?

Do I need to ask for or grant forgiveness for my actions or attitudes this week?

Was my level of hydration adequate?

Did I practice sound nutrition, including vitamins and high-quality foods?

Have I kept something to myself that should be discussed with my sponsor, advisor or therapist?

What areas of my life need improvement?

What service did I perform to help another or my group?

What was my major character flaw this week?

What was my most admirable trait this week?

Did I practice restraint of tongue and pen?

Did I rationalize any destructive behavior?

What are the corrective actions that need to be taken based on this week's inventory? Do I owe any amends?

Abstinent Through Illness

How do we survive the flu and stay abstinent? Remember: Abstinence is a priority. The flu will be gone in a week or two, but food addiction is not going away.

How should we guard our recovery during a bout of illness?

Don't use food to medicate. Refuse soda crackers and ginger ale.

Stay on your scheduled food plan whether hungry or not.

Select appetizing foods.

Try homemade chicken soup with weighed and measured ingredients.

Put breakfast ingredients in the blender to make a smoothie.

Call for help if you need it.

Keep drinking water. Hydration is crucial during illness.

To be sure medications are sugar- and alcohol-free, check inactive ingredients. Discuss with doctor and pharmacist.

Remember cough drops are candy in disguise, and "syrup" means "sugar."

Try the health food store for helpful products to relieve symptoms. Check ingredients on these products too.

Use the phone to maintain contacts and to substitute for missed meetings.

∽◦∾

Affirmation: Abstinence first!

Reflection: Have I prepared ahead for the challenges of flu season by finding ways to care for myself while protecting my abstinence?

Putting on the Gloves

A friend shares, "My disease is like a boxer in a boxing ring, always ready to go at it with me. Anytime I choose to pick up the gloves and get in the ring, I get my tush kicked! For today, I am not going in the ring. I am staying here, in abstinence, instead."

Our disease has lots of ways to put on the gloves that will start that fight up all over again. Careless abstinence puts us back in the boxing ring. Any lapse in recovery routines will resume the struggle.

Paying attention to warnings of relapse will keep us out of the ring. Remembering that the disease is a no-win situation keeps us on our toes.

—∞—

Affirmation: *I stick with the winners.*

Reflection: *How can I incorporate all of my recovery aids to keep me in the winners' circle?*

Change

What word do you think of when you think about the word "change"? Nine times out of ten, the idea of change produces a negative response.

Changing is difficult, scary, stressful and hard work. We don't know what is going to unfold. However, growth, transformation and reaching our potential all involve change *and* resistance. Resistance to change is harmful and usually automatic, while accepting and adapting to change is beneficial and takes effort.

The status quo is so comfy. We just love it. Yet, whether we like it or not, change happens. In fact, change is the only thing we can count on. Change is a constant.

Acceptance is one of the major lessons we learn in recovery. As we change and grow in recovery, we learn to embrace the present, and we accept new ideas. Every stage of recovery has opportunities, challenges and surprises. We have the choice to resist or enjoy the changes. What a choice!

∽o∾

Affirmation: I easily make the changes that move me forward.

Reflection: Do I see change as exciting and challenging and the way to move ahead?

No Reservations

How about this attitude? "There is no playing around with my program. It is what I do, period. It doesn't make any difference if it is sunny or rainy, if I am happy or not, if I am too busy or feeling sick, if I am home or on vacation, I just do it, every day. It is who I am and what I do to live my life happy, joyous and free."

Can you imagine the person who said that having a surprise relapse? I don't think so. In this statement, we find commitment, deliberate intention and the discipline to gain and maintain abstinent recovery.

∽o∽

Affirmation: I affirm recovery every day in every way!

Reflection: Have I fit my life into recovery or recovery into my life?

The Practice of Rigorous Honesty

Dishonesty ensures failure.

Today's headlines are filled with news of the mighty brought down by deceitful dealings. Dishonesty creates a stressful life of confusion. Just remembering and keeping track of all the lies we tell creates havoc. Liars are mistrusted and don't trust others.

Honesty is so simple. There is nothing to think about—just straightforward living. No lying, cheating or stealing means no guilt, fear or shame. We can become our authentic selves starting with self-honesty. Our step work introduces us to honesty and keeps us there.

∞

Affirmation: Honesty is the peaceful, simple way for me.

Reflection: Today I will take an "honesty inventory," starting with a list entitled "Things I Am Dishonest About." For each item listed, I will develop an intervention with the help of my sponsor.

Let Us Write and Reflect on
the Following Question

∽∾

When do I experience the greatest happiness in my life?

_____

_____

_____

_____

_____

_____

_____

_____

_____

_____

_____

_____

_____

_____

_____

Let Us Write and Reflect
on the Past Week

Did I attend an adequate number of meetings?

Did I exercise too little or too much?

Did I take a Tenth Step inventory on a daily basis?

Was I accountable and honest about my food planning and implementation?

What steps did I practice?

Was I resentful, angry, selfish, dishonest or fearful?

Was I generous, kind, tolerant, patient or useful?

Were my actions, words or communications unloving or unkind?

Do I need to ask for or grant forgiveness for my actions or attitudes this week?

Was my level of hydration adequate?

Did I practice sound nutrition, including vitamins and high-quality foods?

Have I kept something to myself that should be discussed with my sponsor, advisor or therapist?

What areas of my life need improvement?

What service did I perform to help another or my group?

What was my major character flaw this week?

What was my most admirable trait this week?

Did I practice restraint of tongue and pen?

Did I rationalize any destructive behavior?

What are the corrective actions that need to be taken based on this week's inventory? Do I owe any amends?

Rest, Relax, Renew

HALT reminds us not to get too hungry, angry, lonely, tired—all conditions that lead to thoughts of food for relief.

I know someone with a powerful, committed recovery plan, but she gets no rest. Rest and relaxation must be built into the recovery plan. Every healthy choice supports good recovery. Rest and relaxation are healthy choices.

When we were full of sugar and caffeine, we had no idea we were tired. We woke up with coffee and passed out from starches. Feeling agitated or lethargic, we never enjoyed a sense of physical well-being.

If insomnia is a problem, search for alternatives to addictive sleeping pills. Make good rest, sleep and relaxation a priority. Take the healthy choice.

∽∘∾

Affirmation: Good rest and sleep promote healing, health and well-being.

Reflection: Do I get to bed at a reasonable time, take a relaxation break during the day and get some exercise that will enhance my sleep?

Let Us Write and Reflect on
the Following Idea

ဟာ

My life is a performance for which I was never given any chance to rehearse.

Ashleigh Brilliant, *Potshots No. 1318*

_____

_____

_____

_____

_____

_____

_____

_____

_____

_____

_____

_____

_____

_____

Nostalgic Memories

Nostalgic memories can create high-risk situations. We are tempted to think back to the good old holiday foods and drinks of the past, while forgetting the sick feelings at the end of the day.

Last night a recovering friend was speaking of a Thanksgiving before recovery. He described his huge table set beautifully with crystal, china and silver. Family and friends had come from all over the country to celebrate with him. The day ended when he found himself throwing suitcases out into the street, cursing and screaming, "Don't ever come back!"

Before the next bite of addictive food, we must remember the consequences of our last binge!

∽◦∽

Affirmation: *Today is the best day of all.*

Reflection: *Have I examined nostalgic memories honestly, remembering with accuracy the consequences of addictive eating and drinking?*

Happy Holidays!

One of the obvious pitfalls of the holiday season is the abundance of tempting food and drink. Magazine covers display the foods that trigger our addiction and our life of horror in innocent and gorgeous splendor. The whole world has missed the idea that those foods should be photographed with a skull-and-crossbones "poison" label.

For those of us who are predisposed to addiction, holiday foods are particularly devastating. Of course, some folks are always urging us to eat "just a little" of those foods. Or worse yet, others offer to prepare abstinent food for us, but then we show up for dinner to find nothing for us to eat. Some hostesses even lie about the ingredients, thinking they can "put one over on us."

The best way to maintain abstinence throughout the holiday orgy of addictive substances is to eliminate and restrict the number of occasions attended, show up prepared with our own food or eat before the party.

∽○∽

Affirmation: I maintain abstinence through the holidays by thoughtful planning.

Reflection: Have I planned my party options carefully in order to maintain abstinence?

Risky Business

Some people can prepare addictive trigger foods and stay safe, but why do it?

Just today we heard from a friend who took a taste while preparing her child's (far from abstinent) lunch. Baking, cooking, storing and touching poisonous foods is a danger that must be reconsidered.

Why continue to push drugs? Improve the nutritional level of the household and offer wholesome food to the family. They may not want to eat exactly what we eat, but most of our foods are fine for them. Who would turn away a steak, baked potato and salad? Let's avoid handling foods that destroy us. At least let the kids make their own lunches.

∽o∾

Affirmation: My food choices are healthy and wholesome.

Reflection: Am I willing to prepare safe, nourishing food for the family?

Think Twice

No problem is so bad that we can't find a way to make it worse. In the past, I have had a gut-level feeling that I should retreat, while watching my self march forward into self-destruction. It was like an out-of-body experience; I watched as I made the worst possible choice.

Making our problems worse is a common practice for addicts. We lack life skills. Often we think about doing something effective, while doing otherwise.

A slogan poster in some meeting rooms says, "Think, Think, Think." That's three times! It means to think before we eat, drink, act out or make matters worse.

The next step to that operation is to pay attention to the thought. Usually a really good one comes up, so we take heed and follow our best inclinations. And remember, we need our sponsor's input too!

᠂ᡂᢁ

Affirmation: I think it through before making a decision.

Reflection: In what ways can I avoid impulsive reactions?

Let Us Write and Reflect
on the Past Week

᠊ᡣᠣᡣ᠊

Did I attend an adequate number of meetings?

Did I exercise too little or too much?

Did I take a Tenth Step inventory on a daily basis?

Was I accountable and honest about my food planning and implementation?

What steps did I practice?

Was I resentful, angry, selfish, dishonest or fearful?

Was I generous, kind, tolerant, patient or useful?

Were my actions, words or communications unloving or unkind?

Do I need to ask for or grant forgiveness for my actions or attitudes this week?

Was my level of hydration adequate?

Did I practice sound nutrition, including vitamins and high quality foods?

Have I kept something to myself that should be discussed with my sponsor, advisor or therapist?

What areas of my life need improvement?

What service did I perform to help another or my group?

What was my major character flaw this week?

What was my most admirable trait this week?

Did I practice restraint of tongue and pen?

Did I rationalize any destructive behavior?

What are the corrective actions that need to be taken based on this week's inventory? Do I owe any amends?

Can't Have

Often people ask if they "can have" a particular food, or is such-and-such a food "allowed." I answer, "You can have anything you want. However, that food is not on the food plan." This program isn't about what we can and can't have; the program is about choosing. We can choose whether to abstain or not abstain, and we make that daily choice based on our level of spiritual commitment.

What would happen if I said, "You can't have that food"? The person would react with anger and rebellion. No one can decide what another person can or cannot eat.

Providing good information does not include making rules and regulations for others to follow. That information can be used or rejected. That's why we call them guidelines, not requirements.

ㅇㅇ

Affirmation: *I make healthy food choices based on trustworthy guidelines.*

Reflection: *Do I make use of good information for change and growth?*

Did I Really Let Go?

Today I turned my life and will over to God, made a list of things I worried about, turned my worries over to God, made a list of things that irritated me and turned my irritations over to God. When will I surrender my entire life and will over to the care of God? All the time! Letting go is a lifelong enterprise.

∽o∽

Affirmation: *I practice spiritual surrender.*

Reflection: *Since surrender is unending, what have I surrendered today?*

Simplicity

A friend lamented, "A Twelve Step program and weighing and measuring isn't what I would have chosen as a spiritual path. I would have preferred some kind of funky, cool solution, like a sojourn to Tibet every year."

Our program is much simpler than that. Recovery comes down to two concepts: The first is "Do it" and the second is "Don't do it."

On the Do It list, we find the recovery actions that our friend mentions, our Twelve Step program with an effective food plan.

On the *Don't* Do It list, we record all of the temptations that will undermine our program.

Our path is so simple. When we are happy, healthy and whole, then we can sojourn to Tibet if we wish.

సోయ

Affirmation: *The things I need to do turn out to be the things I want to do.*

Reflection: *Does my plan consist of two lists: things to do and behaviors to avoid?*

Grace: God's Love for Me

I will never forget the moment of grace that turned around my life of food addiction. There I stood with a box of sweets in my hands and realized for the first time in my life that something was wrong with my relationship to that candy.

Nothing was different that day. I was sneaking, hiding and eating someone else's food just as I had since early childhood. As I stood there, at that particular moment in time, my delusions were smashed. I could see clearly the selfishness and compulsion of my food addiction. I had never seen it before.

Looking back at that moment, I know that I was filled with the grace of God. My denial and delusions were displaced by clarity of mind and the understanding that my relationship with food was abnormal. There was no wondering what to do about this addiction. Several weeks earlier I had been invited to a meeting for food addicts. I was all set to go, as the grace of God delivered me from food addiction.

∽○∽

Affirmation: *I trust the love of God to deliver me from food addiction.*

Reflection: *Do I recognize the opportunities God sends to me?*

Attainable Affirmations:
Accountability

To whom are we accountable and for what? Personal accountability comes from within. Blame, complaints and procrastination are eliminated when we accept responsibility for our goals, actions and decisions as they affect our recovery and ultimately our lives. We build in a process of accountability in our recovery plan, using a sponsor in order to ensure a greater degree of adherence.

∽o∾

I accept responsibility for my recovery.
I honestly communicate with my sponsor.
My recovery is a cherished responsibility.

Successful Twelve Step Work

Consider the various ways we "carry the message to the still-suffering food addict." We attend meetings, sharing our experience, strength and hope before, during and after. Sponsoring, telephoning, encouraging, supporting and sharing rides to meetings with other recovering food addicts are all Step Twelve actions. Working with others, we hope and pray that the newcomer and the "retread" will make it.

How can we tell if we are successful? If we stay abstinent, we have been successful. We come to realize that the recovery actions we take are for ourselves. We can't keep it unless we give it away!

∽∘∾

Affirmation: I reinforce my recovery by sharing with a newer person.

Reflection: Have I realized that when I put my hand out to help another food addict, I am doing it for my own survival?

Stick with the Winners.
Win with the Stickers

Identifying a winner is the first item on this agenda. Who is a winner anyway? Someone who has achieved lasting and meaningful recovery, a person who is strong in their intent to accomplish and enjoy the process of recovery.

A winner . . .

has completed the steps.

has a wise and commonsense approach to life.

maintains abstinence.

does service work.

attends meetings regularly.

is available.

practices gratitude and acceptance.

When you find this winner, stick with him or her. We can use all of the winners we can find in our support system. They give us courage, confidence and the realization that recovery is possible!

∽o∾

Affirmation: I stick with the winners.

Reflection: Today I will phone the winners who support me and thank them for being there.

Practice These Principles

Think of the story of the violinist who knew the way to avoid failure. He said, "If I fail to practice for even one day, I can tell the difference. If I fail to practice for two days, my family will see the difference. If I fail to practice three days, the whole world will know."

We fail when we quit practicing. We are charged in Step Twelve to "practice these principles in all our affairs." Just learning them is not enough. We must practice them on a daily basis—over and over again—in *all* our affairs.

People who accomplish unconditional abstinence—staying abstinent in every situation and under all circumstances—practice these principles. Practice makes permanent. When we practice the principles of recovery, the whole world will know!

∽∘∾

Affirmation: I practice spiritual principles in all of my associations.

Reflection: Have I studied the principles embodied in the Twelve Steps? They are honesty, acceptance, hope, faith, courage, integrity, willingness, humility, love, self-discipline, perseverance, devotion and service.

Intention

When intention wanes, then chaos reigns.

Elsa M. Glover

Intention is an important aspect of recovery, setting into motion the whole recovery process. When our intentions are clear and focused, a predictable outcome will result.

After a recent meeting, a friend who attends meetings daily said, "Those people in relapse wonder why they are having so much trouble. I don't see them at very many meetings." We might guess that people who are not present at meetings have conflicting intentions. The intention to rest or watch television may overcome the intention to attend a meeting. When the intention to recover wanes, chaos in the form of relapse will reign—guaranteed!

Intention to recover must not waver. Like a horse in blinders, we look straight ahead, focused on abstinence and growth.

∽o∾

Affirmation: I do not falter in my intention to put recovery first.

Reflection: In what ways do I put recovery first? In what ways do I fail to do so?

My Best Teacher

We are surrounded by teachers. Our best teacher is the guy or gal that we are the most upset with right now. How can that be? A spiritual leader would seem to serve as a better guide.

Let's say we are hopping mad at a relative. The anger is a loud messenger that a lesson is waiting to be learned.

Although our anger seems justified, the real cause of our distress is losing connection with our Higher Power. Anger takes us out of our place of peace and puts us into spiritual chaos.

The relative we are upset with is not the problem. We have put something we want and expect from them ahead of our love for them. At that exact moment, we lose love. Returning to love is simple: We give up our demands and affirm our love and acceptance of our relative.

∽o∾

Affirmation: I keep love current by eliminating expectations.

Reflection: Have I learned that when expectations are high, serenity is low?

Patience

We may think about patience as a goal. *If I do this, this and this,* we think, we will become more patient, which would be a good thing to accomplish. Is patience a virtue to be practiced and developed or the consequence of right thinking?

Let's see how we create impatience. Here comes someone into the express lane at the grocery store with fifteen articles in his basket. The sign clearly says ten. *Well, durn his hide, can't the fool read? Guess he can't count either. Wouldn't you know I would get behind this guy when I am in the biggest hurry? I would be first in line if he hadn't wandered into the wrong line. Omigosh, he is writing a check too. There should be guards by these lines directing people who won't pay attention.* You bet I am impatient, my thoughts are creating it.

I could create peaceful, loving patience by saying, "Bless him, change me."

∽◦∾

Affirmation: I see the innocence of others by abolishing negative thoughts about them.

Reflection: How can I use grocery store lanes as my spiritual path?

Don't Answer That Phone!

Here's a new idea: When the phone rings, we don't have to answer it. When the machine takes the message, we don't have to return the call. Whatever comes our way, we have a choice to accept or reject it.

Responding to the requests of others, whether they arrive in the form of phone calls or by other routes, is not mandatory. We can make a choice, take charge, be an actor or a reactor. We can choose to respond to the request, refuse the request or schedule it for another time. Exercising our choice can keep us from being resentful and overcommitted, and feeling used and abused.

∽∘∾

Affirmation: I enjoy the structure of a manageable schedule.

Reflection: Have I taken charge of my schedule by deciding a convenient time to answer phone calls?

Complacency

A major cause of relapse has a name: complacency. Relapse takes no effort, while recovery requires consistent participation.

Relapse is what happens in the absence of a strong recovery program. There are no holidays from recovery. We are either going forward or backward. When life gets better, we are tempted by other undertakings, art classes, church activities, sports, theatre and more responsibilities at work. All worthwhile pastimes, these! We can rest on our laurels. After all, that's why we got abstinent, so we can have a better life. Right?

The groundless idea here is that successful abstinence cancels the need for additional effort. We become abstinent to have a better life, and we *stay* abstinent for the same reason. When the "good life" crowds out program obligations, the disease will take over promptly.

∽∾

Affirmation: I stay abstinent and enjoy a better life.

Reflection: Do I resist complacency by making time for all of my recovery needs?

Let Us Write and Reflect
on the Past Week

∽∘∾

Did I attend an adequate number of meetings?

Did I exercise too little or too much?

Did I take a Tenth Step inventory on a daily basis?

Was I accountable and honest about my food planning and implementation?

What steps did I practice?

Was I resentful, angry, selfish, dishonest or fearful?

Was I generous, kind, tolerant, patient or useful?

Were my actions, words or communications unloving or unkind?

Do I need to ask for or grant forgiveness for my actions or attitudes this week?

Was my level of hydration adequate?

Did I practice sound nutrition, including vitamins and high-quality foods?

Have I kept something to myself that should be discussed with my sponsor, advisor or therapist?

What areas of my life need improvement?

What service did I perform to help another or my group?

What was my major character flaw this week?

What was my most admirable trait this week?

Did I practice restraint of tongue and pen?

Did I rationalize any destructive behavior?

What are the corrective actions that need to be taken based on this week's inventory? Do I owe any amends?

The Twelve Steps are the spiritual principles that guide us in our personal recovery. The founders of AA came up with twelve principles—Traditions—that keep our groups intact. These Twelve Traditions are to the groups what the Twelve Steps are to the individual. They are suggested principles that ensure the survival and growth of the group. Hammered out on the anvil of experience, they were designed to guide our groups. Personal survival and survival of our program depend on understanding and implementing these principles. We need to develop a personal regard for the Twelve Traditions and an awareness of our role in preserving the unity of our Twelve Step program. In recovery, we become practitioners of the Twelve Steps *and* the Twelve Traditions.

TRADITION TWELVE

"Anonymity is the spiritual foundation of all our traditions, ever reminding us to place principles before personalities."

Anonymity is the spiritual basis of all the Traditions. Principles take precedence over personal interests.

All of the Traditions are reminders that we are no longer going to do it "our way." To express the principles embodied in the Traditions, we learn to let go.

In *Tradition One,* we let go of personal desires by placing the common good first.

Tradition Two challenges us to let go of self-will by seeking God's will spoken through our group's conscience.

We abandon safeguards, rules and regulations with *Tradition Three:* Membership requires only "the desire to stop eating addictively."

By *Tradition Four* we discard the concept of authority and governing from the "top down" in favor of group autonomy.

Tradition Five encourages us to give up personal agendas by restricting group focus to carrying the message to other food addicts.

Tradition Six encourages us to let go of power, materialism and personal status-seeking in favor of "our primary purpose" of carrying the message.

Tradition Seven says that we pay our own bills and give up any idea of "outside contributions."

To practice the *Eighth Tradition,* we surrender the idea of compensation for our Twelve Step work in order to express love without a price tag.

Tradition Nine encourages responsible service, not costly organization.

Tradition Ten reminds us that controversy will destroy us.

Tradition Eleven advises that we give up self-promotion in favor of humility and anonymity.

Tradition Twelve incorporates the principles of the preceding traditions. Unity is the goal of all these.

∽○∾

Affirmation: *Unity, recovery and service are my goals.*

Reflection: *Today I will reflect on the principles embodied in the Twelve Traditions.*

God's Way Versus the World's Way

Nothing counts in this world but God's will. St. Augustine said, "Love God, then do what you will." If we come from a place of love for God, how can we err?

My friend has had a terrible time in extensive relapse, suffering tremendous weight gains, as well as great personal and financial losses. Back on the food plan, she admitted that she had considered bypass surgery. However, she declined that option saying, "It isn't spiritual. Recovery is the spiritual path for me." Heeding the will of God for her, she deliberately chose the way of spiritual growth.

The source of our ultimate victory over food addiction is through unconditional surrender to God's will. Such faith leads to liberation and the enjoyment of all of God's gifts.

∽∘∾

Affirmation: *I have surrendered myself to the love of God.*

Reflection: *Where will I find ultimate victory over food addiction?*

War or Peace?

Two things give me great peace. The first is to resist defending my position. The second is to decline arguing against another's beliefs. Although I am happy to share my point of view, I have no need to persuade anyone to accept it. I am equally happy to allow people their own opinion.

∽◦∽

Affirmation: I strive to see other people's point of view.

Reflection: Have I found the way to eliminate defensive behaviors?

Greater Power

Our understanding of a Higher Power is up to us. . . .
The only suggested guidelines are that this Power
be loving, caring and greater than ourselves.

Narcotics Anonymous, p. 24

The guidance offered in the N.A. basic text is well-founded. So many suffering addicts have arrived with a different idea of God or no view at all. What a comfort to be guided to find a loving, caring Greater Power. At our lowest point in our illness, desperately needing that loving care, we are pointed toward this healing faith.

∽◦∽

Affirmation: *My Higher Power is the greatest power in my life.*

Reflection: *Am I grateful for the loving, caring Higher Power that I have found in recovery?*

One Good Idea

Would you like to know how to make every meeting a rousing success? Look for one good idea to take home from the meeting. In my early days in recovery, I would memorize one thought from each meeting to use as a recovery slogan to help me through the week. We might even go further and look for a good idea from each of the members attending the meeting. The result? Looking for the positives will result in a upbeat attitude about meetings while our enjoyment of them grows.

∽o∾

Affirmation: I look for positive helpful ideas at my recovery meetings.

Reflection: Start a list of original slogans gleaned from meeting shares. Hang posters or post notes with these ideas in strategic places as recovery reminders.

Today's Stress Buster:
Simplify Meals

Here are a few ways to simplify meals:

Eat two cups of cooked vegetables at lunch and two cups of raw vegetables for dinner. This cuts vegetable prep time in half.

Eat the same protein and starch for breakfast, lunch and dinner.

When preparing a meal, make a second one for the freezer.

Save small amounts of potatoes to supplement if one is too small.

Freeze small portions of all kinds of leftover beans in a bag. Keep adding until there is a full cup. This results in a nice variety of beans for a soup or salad.

Weigh and measure grain and protein portions and keep in the freezer for quick and easy meals.

Let Us Write and Reflect
on the Past Week

❦

Did I attend an adequate number of meetings?

Did I exercise too little or too much?

Did I take a Tenth Step inventory on a daily basis?

Was I accountable and honest about my food planning and implementation?

What steps did I practice?

Was I resentful, angry, selfish, dishonest or fearful?

Was I generous, kind, tolerant, patient or useful?

Were my actions, words or communications unloving or unkind?

Do I need to ask for or grant forgiveness for my actions or attitudes this week?

Was my level of hydration adequate?

Did I practice sound nutrition, including vitamins and high-quality foods?

Have I kept something to myself that should be discussed with my sponsor, advisor or therapist?

What areas of my life need improvement?

What service did I perform to help another or my group?

What was my major character flaw this week?

What was my most admirable trait this week?

Did I practice restraint of tongue and pen?

Did I rationalize any destructive behavior?

What are the corrective actions that need to be taken based on this week's inventory? Do I owe any amends?

Let Us Write and Reflect on
the Following Question

∽o∾

What does relaxation mean to me?

_____

_____

_____

_____

_____

_____

_____

_____

_____

_____

_____

_____

_____

_____

_____

Prayer of St. Francis

Make me a channel of your peace.
Where there is hatred let me bring your love.
Where there is injury, your pardon, Lord,
And where there's doubt, true faith in you.
Make me a channel of your peace.
Where there's despair in life, let me bring hope.
Where there is darkness, only light.
And where there's sadness, ever joy.
Oh, Master, grant that I may never seek
So much to be consoled as to console,
To be understood as to understand.
To be loved as to love with all my soul.
Make me a channel of your peace.
It is in pardoning that we are pardoned.
In giving of ourselves that we receive,
And in dying that we're born to eternal life.

~∞~

Affirmation: God makes me a channel of His peace.

Reflection: In what ways is a peaceful life my personal choice? Do I promote peace or turmoil?

Taking It Personally

*Don't take anything personally
because by taking things personally you set
yourself up to suffer for nothing.*

Don Miguel Ruiz, *The Four Agreements*, p. 56

After presenting in a workshop on the subject of Don't Take Things Personally, I had one woman come forward, look me straight in the eyes and say forcefully, "No matter what you say, it is *always* about me." She's fun (and just a tad self-absorbed).

In her case, it was funny. However, taking things personally is not the way to joy and happiness. When someone calls us dumb, fat or ugly, we don't have to take it personally.

If someone called us a "chair," would we care? Of course not. What other people think of us is none of our business. Their comment comes from their lack of love. It is not about us at all.

❧

Affirmation: *Today I don't take anything personally.*

Reflection: *When I am unloved by others, do I see that it is their problem, not mine?*

Let Us Write and Reflect on
the Following Idea

∾∾

Gradually, we stop trying to bargain, plead and bribe God for an obstacle-free life, and we accept life on life's terms. As we recognize God's mercy and love toward us by allowing us another chance, we become more merciful and loving toward others. We peek outside our narcissism and feel genuine concern for our fellow humans.

Judy Shepps-Battle

Doing the Next Right Thing

I had to make amends today. Even harder than that, I had to set some boundaries. It felt like a moral root canal.

Yesterday, I became angry and hung up on an in-law. I had done this once before several years ago. I had made amends to her in the past and waded right back into it with her again. Today, it was lurking in the back of my mind, chipping away at my peace and contentment. I honestly didn't want to make amends. I wanted relief, but I liked being estranged from her. Well, God sent the troops in to do the job.

First, the phone rang. It was my sponsor. She was driving to the airport and had lots of time to kill on her cell phone. After we caught up on the day-to-day things we usually talk about, I told her about my discomfort. The decision was made! I would write and mail an amends letter right away—no phone calls allowed.

Just as I hung up, the doorbell rang and in came the rest of the solution. An enlightened Al-Anon lady was at the door to pick up some books. She had time to come in and sit for a while. I told her I had some amends to make and told her about the lesson I was working on. She exclaimed, "You don't owe amends, you need to set boundaries." *Oh no,* said the disease in me, *I don't wanna!* Although I had made amends in the past, I hadn't finished my work. It became so clear as I spoke to my Al-Anon friend that I had to set boundaries with this in-law. That is my responsibility.

So I wrote the letter, said I was sorry for my attitude and actions, and then spelled out the exact boundaries that fit the situation, knowing that I was cutting off a source of information that kept me in codependent's hell.

Because I have turned my life and my will over to my Higher Power, He is in charge. He sends the troops in when I need them the most. I know why the phone and the doorbell rang. It was God calling.

∾o∾

Affirmation: *God's spirit in me accomplishes miracles around me.*

Reflection: *Am I willing to do the next right thing because I like the results?*

Carrying the Message

Our great wealth is recovery. It is ours to give freely to help others. The freedom to give away our wealth is our greatest satisfaction.

People who have suffered from addiction have been carrying the message of recovery since the early 1930s. In meeting rooms and diners and across kitchen tables, the message of hope has been shared from one addict to another—a message that has turned lives from despair to triumph. With singleness of purpose, our entire fellowship exists to communicate the good news of recovery.

❧

Affirmation: *I gladly spread the wealth of recovery.*

Reflection: *In what ways do I communicate to other food addicts the message of recovery?*

Let Us Write and Reflect
on the Past Week

∽o∾

Did I attend an adequate number of meetings?

Did I exercise too little or too much?

Did I take a Tenth Step inventory on a daily basis?

Was I accountable and honest about my food planning and implementation?

What steps did I practice?

Was I resentful, angry, selfish, dishonest or fearful?

Was I generous, kind, tolerant, patient or useful?

Were my actions, words or communications unloving or unkind?

Do I need to ask for or grant forgiveness for my actions or attitudes this week?

Was my level of hydration adequate?

Did I practice sound nutrition, including vitamins and high-quality foods?

Have I kept something to myself that should be discussed with my sponsor, advisor or therapist?

What areas of my life need improvement?

What service did I perform to help another or my group?

What was my major character flaw this week?

What was my most admirable trait this week?

Did I practice restraint of tongue and pen?

Did I rationalize any destructive behavior?

What are the corrective actions that need to be taken based on this week's inventory? Do I owe any amends?

A True Story

A member of a recovery group shares how one woman's support network came through for her.

One of the group's members was admitted to the hospital. She called her sponsor, who called several others who all went into action. Her husband helped her advocate for no dextrose drips. Her team of helpers made sure that no sugar was going to get into their friend's body. One member brought lunch and dinner on the second day. Another brought two coolers full of food, a scale, measuring cups, spoons, sea salt and sweetener. Someone else prepared her metabolic for her. They labeled all of her food, made a list for her and talked with the nurses. On the third day, she ate food prepared by her fellow members the entire day. On the fourth day, she had safe proteins and vegetables from the hospital for lunch and dinner, and her breakfast, metabolic and grains were provided by the recovery team.

One of the team members shares, "I tell you, this was such a rewarding experience. I feel like a pioneer for food addiction. The nurses were confused at first, but my sponsor and I kept firm in our resolve to see that our friend was protected from the evil addictive substances."

∽∘∾

Affirmation: I love and support others through tough times.

Reflection: Am I willing to advocate for other food addicts who can't provide for themselves?

The Greatest Gift of All

Did you ever see a child receive a gift and enjoy the wrapping and the carton more than what's inside? He doesn't understand the value of the contents of the package. It is all the same to him.

Sometimes we do the same thing in recovery. We become enamored with the wrappings of our recovery. We love our weight loss, improved family relations, better health, greater job performance and financial security. All are wonderful gifts, but they are the wrappings. Deep in the box lies the real gift: our relationship with God.

As for me, I want the whole package! I want to reach deeply into my recovery gift box to enjoy my friendship with God.

∽∾∾

Affirmation: Recovery is a gift, and I want the whole package.

Reflection: Have I been distracted by the wrappings of recovery, especially physical improvements?

A Lifetime Program,
One Day at a Time

No mandatory retirement age applies to the recovering food addict. Although life comes to us in daily portions, the lessons will appear for the rest of our lives.

For the duration of our lifetime, we will either grow or decline spiritually. At every age and stage of our lives, we have the capacity to grow and change. We are the lucky ones who have a program that promotes that growth. The challenge is to keep our program active, enthusiastic and progressive, no matter how long we have been around.

∽∘∾

Affirmation: I would rather be green and growing than ripe and rotting!

Reflection: Do I keep my program green, fresh and new?

Misfortune/Good Fortune

The downward spiral of addiction is a horrifying process. Recalling the agony of the progression and the fact that being a food addict is a blessing seems strange. Addiction, though, provided the opportunity for great good fortune: a spiritual way of living.

∽∘∾

Affirmation: *Addiction has been my greatest gift.*

Reflection: *Do I see the gifts I have received as I watch with awe the amazing progression of recovery?*

A Spiritual Axiom

It is a spiritual axiom that every time
we are disturbed, no matter what the cause,
there is something wrong with us.

Twelve Steps and Twelve Traditions, p. 90

Great personal power resides in that truth. Recognizing that something is wrong with us gives us the power to correct that wrong. We find out what the problem is and change it. Simple, but not easy. These simple facts provide us with our lifetime occupation: evaluating and correcting those wrongs.

❧

Affirmation: *I continue to take personal inventory and when I am wrong promptly admit it.*

Reflection: *Do I recognize the subtle wrongs as well as the obvious ones?*

Today's Stress Buster:
Employ Your Sense of Humor

A laugh is a great stress buster! You can find a laugh in most everything. Humor is a healthy way of putting a problem in perspective.

For those who wish to be mentally healthy, a recovery saying is, "Humor is our best friend, temper is our worst enemy." When we choose a laugh, a smile or a joke instead of a tantrum or a breakdown, we are rewarded with better health: mental, physical and spiritual.

Jonathan Swift wrote: "The best doctors in the world are Dr. Diet, Dr. Quiet and Dr. Merryman," translated to food plan, quiet time and humor—all recovery aids.

Let Us Write and Reflect
on the Past Week

಄

Did I attend an adequate number of meetings?

Did I exercise too little or too much?

Did I take a Tenth Step inventory on a daily basis?

Was I accountable and honest about my food planning and implementation?

What steps did I practice?

Was I resentful, angry, selfish, dishonest or fearful?

Was I generous, kind, tolerant, patient or useful?

Were my actions, words or communications unloving or unkind?

Do I need to ask for or grant forgiveness for my actions or attitudes this week?

Was my level of hydration adequate?

Did I practice sound nutrition, including vitamins and high-quality foods?

Have I kept something to myself that should be discussed with my sponsor, advisor or therapist?

What areas of my life need improvement?

What service did I perform to help another or my group?

What was my major character flaw this week?

What was my most admirable trait this week?

Did I practice restraint of tongue and pen?

Did I rationalize any destructive behavior?

What are the corrective actions that need to be taken based on this week's inventory? Do I owe any amends?

Attainable Affirmations:
Good-Bye to the Past

The past is filled with regrets. Recovery practice leads us out of the past and into the present. Inventory and amends heal our pasts. When we use our rearview mirror, we focus on what's behind us but we miss what is in front of us. For a healthy mind and body, the secret is letting go of past regrets to live prudently in the present. Without regrets, remember the past, learn from it and move on. The present holds countless possibilities.

∽⚬∽

The past has no power; I release it forever.
I let go of past mistakes and worries forever.
I accept the goodness of the present.
And so it is.

The Twelve Steps for Food Addicts

1. We admitted we were powerless over addictive foods — that our lives had become unmanageable.
2. Came to believe that a Power greater than ourselves could restore us to sanity.
3. Made a decision to turn our will and our lives over to the care of God as we understood Him.
4. Made a searching and fearless moral inventory of ourselves.
5. Admitted to God, to ourselves and to another human being the exact nature of our wrongs.
6. Were entirely ready to have God remove all these defects of character.
7. Humbly asked Him to remove our shortcomings.
8. Made a list of all persons we had harmed, and became willing to make amends to them all.
9. Made direct amends to such people wherever possible, except when to do so would injure them or others.
10. Continued to take personal inventory and when we were wrong promptly admitted it.
11. Sought through prayer and meditation to improve our conscious contact with God as we understood Him, praying only for knowledge of His will for us and the power to carry that out.
12. Having had a spiritual awakening as the result of these Steps, we tried to carry this message to food addicts, and to practice these principles in all our affairs.

The Abstinent Food Plan

Recovery Food Plan

Here is the most up-to-date food plan formulated for food addiction recovery. Be sure you review this revised version even if you are an experienced user of the food plan. You may discover that there are new refinements. This plan is based on the concept of abstinence from all foods which will trigger cravings. Abstinence is the foundation of recovery upon which physical, emotional and spiritual growth is built.

Before using this or any other food plan, be sure to check with your doctor for approval.

DAILY PORTIONS

Breakfast

One fruit
One protein
One dairy
One grain

Lunch/Dinner

One protein
One raw vegetable
One cooked vegetable
One starch or grain

Before Bed

One fruit
One dairy

Daily

One fat

Daily Options

Spice, one tablespoon
Sugar-free condiments, two
    tablespoons
Sweeteners, six servings*
Sugar-free broth, one cup

*Note: Exclude sweeteners which contain dextrose, maltodextrose or poly-
    dextrose. This includes all packets. Saccharin and liquid saccharin
    can be used with this plan. Read the warning on the label.

WOMEN'S PORTION SIZES

Protein: four ounces (two eggs)
Starch: one cup (eight ounces potato)
Vegetable: (one cup)
Fruit: six ounces
Dairy: one cup
Cottage cheese: one-half cup
Fat: one tablespoon or three teaspoons

MEN'S PORTION SIZES

Protein: six ounces (three eggs)
Starch: one cup (eight ounces potato)
Vegetable: one cup
Fruit: six ounces
Dairy: one cup
Cottage cheese: one-half cup
Fat: two tablespoons or six teaspoons

Maintenance

Most people maintain on the original food plan. If weight loss is too rapid or too extreme, adjust the food plan with the help of an individual experienced in its use and familiar with the recovery formula of the food plan. The most common error made when making additions to the plan involves adding extra dairy and fruit. Since these are high-sugar foods, their addition negatively affects the carbohydrate-protein balance by increasing the sugar content of the food plan. Make additions, one per week, taking at least three weeks to complete the changes, in the following manner:

1. Add one teaspoon of oil to each meal, equaling one additional tablespoon per day.
2. Add one ounce of protein to each meal.

3. Add two ounces of complex carbohydrate (grain or starchy vegetable) to each meal.

Abstinent Food List

PROTEIN—FOUR OUNCES FOR WOMEN, SIX OUNCES FOR MEN, EXCEPTIONS NOTED

Beef (five ounces for men)
Chicken
Cooked beans/legumes
(one cup for women, one
and a half cups for men)
Eggs (two large for women,
three large for men)
Fish
Lamb
Pork
Shellfish
Tempeh
Tofu (eight ounces for
women, twelve ounces for
men)
Turkey
Veal

VEGETABLES—ONE SERVING EQUALS ONE CUP

Artichokes (not marinated in oil)
Asparagus
Bamboo shoots
Beans (green and yellow)
Beets
Bok choy
Broccoli
Brussels sprouts
Cabbage
Carrots
Cauliflower
Celery
Chinese cabbage
Cucumber
Eggplant
Endive
Escarole
Lettuce
Mushrooms
Okra
Onions
Parsley
Peppers
Pickles, dill
Pimentos
Radishes
Romaine lettuce
Rutabaga

Sauerkraut	Tomatoes
Snowpeas	Turnips
Spinach	Water chestnuts
Sprouts	Watercress
Summer squash	Zucchini

FRUIT—ONE SERVING EQUALS SIX OUNCES

Apple	Nectarine
Apricot	Orange
Berries	Peach
Cantaloupe	Pear
Cranberries	Pineapple
Grapefruit	Plum
Honeydew	Rhubarb
Kiwi	Tangerine
Lemon, lime	Watermelon

STARCHES—ONE SERVING EQUALS ONE CUP

All starchy beans and legumes

Acorn, butternut or spaghetti squash, winter squash

Green peas

Potato (eight ounces scale weight)

Yams and sweet potato (eight ounces scale weight)

WHOLE GRAINS

Barley

Brown rice and brown basmati rice

Buckwheat

Oat bran

Oatmeal

GRAINS *(continued)*

Millet	Teff
Quinoa	Whole oats
Rye	
Steel cut oats	

FAT—DAILY SERVING EQUALS ONE TABLESPOON PER DAY

Canola oil   Olive oil

Other oils are acceptable, but we favor olive and canola.

FAT-FREE DAIRY PRODUCTS including milk, plain yogurt, cottage cheese and buttermilk.

ALL SPICES that are free of starch and sugars.

CONDIMENTS such as mustard, horseradish, vinegar and salsa.

Trigger Foods

We abstain from all forms of alcohol, cocoa, chocolate, caffeine, and sweetened products including gum, desserts, yogurt, cough drops, candy, regular sweeteners and artificial sweeteners.

Sugar: We abstain from sugar in all forms. Refer to Appendix I to review the names of sugar. A good rule of thumb: Discard any product that contains ingredients with obscure names, even if that product is labeled sugar-free.

Flour: We abstain from all flours such as corn and cornmeal, wheat, rice, barley, rye and products such as corn chips and tacos. We abstain from corn starch and arrowroot.

Wheat: We abstain from all wheat products, including macaroni, noodles, bread, pizza, crackers, pita, bagels, muffins, shredded wheat, whole grain wheat, wheat flour and modified food starch.

High-fat foods: We abstain from all high-fat foods, including fried food, butter, sour cream, cream cheese, dairy products over 2 percent fat, hard cheese, ricotta cheese, nuts and seeds. Beware of high-fat processed meat products such as hot dogs, ham, bacon and sausage, even if they are sugar-free. These processed meats are often 80 to 90 percent fat. To check the fat content of such products, calculate the percentage of fat. If there are one hundred sixty calories per serving and one hundred twenty calories of fat per serving, one hundred twenty over one hundred sixty equals three-fourths. Therefore the product is 75 percent fat. This would not be a protein product, but an animal fat product unfit for the food plan.

High-sugar fruits: We abstain from high-sugar fruits, including dried fruit, bananas, grapes, cherries, fruit juice, mangos, raisins and high-fat avocados.

Puffed and popped grains: We abstain from puffed and popped grains such as popped corn and puffed cereals. Puffing and popping refines the product. Refinement produces addictive substances.

Suggested Reading

Alcoholics Anonymous, 3rd ed. (New York: Alcoholics Anonymous World Services, Inc., 1976).

Anderson, Greg, *The 22 Non Negotiable Laws of Wellness* (New York: HarperCollins, 1996).

Bellin, Gita, *A Sharing of Completion* (Self Transformation Seminars Ltd., 1983).

As Bill Sees It (New York: Alcoholics Anonymous World Services, Inc., 1967).

Brilliant, Ashleigh. *I Have Abandoned My Search for Truth and Am Now Looking for a Good Fantasy,* Potshots No. 1318 (Santa Barbara, Calif.: Woodbridge Press, 1980).

Collins, Vincent. *Acceptance: The Way to Serenity and Peace of Mind* (St. Meinrad, Ind.: Abbey Press, 1960).

A Course in Miracles (Glen Ellen, Calif.: Foundation for Inner Peace, 1985).

Dr. Bob and the Good Oldtimers (New York: Alcoholics Anonymous World Services, Inc., 1980).

Fox, Emmet. *The Golden Key* (UnityVillage Mo.: School Publishing, 1931).

Gibran, Kahlil. *The Prophet* (New York: Random House, 1923).

Hayden, Ruth. *How to Turn Your Money Life Around* (Deerfield Beach, Fla.: Health Communications, Inc., 1992).

Keyes, Ken. *Handbook to Higher Consciousness,* fifth edition (Kentucky: The Living Love Center, 1975).

Miller, Merlene, Gorski, Terence and Miller, David. *Learning to Live Again* (Independence, Mo.: Independence Press, 1982).

Murray, W. H. *The Scottish Himalayan Expedition* (London: J. H. Dent and Sons, Ltd., 1951).

Narcotics Anonymous (Van Nuys, Calif.: World Services, Inc., 1988).

One Day at a Time in Al-Anon (Virginia Beach, Va.: Al-Anon Family Groups Headquarters, 1989).

Pert, Candace. *Your Body Is Your Subconscious Mind, Study Guide* (Boulder, Colo.: Sounds True, Inc., 2000).

Recovery from Food Addiction Abstinence Guidelines (Houston, Tex.: Recovery from Food Addiction, Inc., 1994).

Ruiz, Don Miguel. *The Four Agreements* (San Rafael, Calif.: Amber-Allen Publishing, 1997).

Ryce, Michael. *Why Is This Happening to Me Again?* (Theodosia, Mo.: Dr. Michael Ryce, 1996).

Sheppard, Kay. *Food Addiction: The Body Knows* (Deerfield Beach, Fla.: Health Communications, Inc., 1993).

————. *From the First Bite* (Deerfield Beach, Fla.: Health Communications, Inc., 2000).

St. Clair-Thomas, John and Lyn, and Steve Shackel. *Eyes of the Beholder* (Goulburn, Australia: Angel Publications, 1982).

Twelve Steps and Twelve Traditions (New York: Alcoholics Anonymous World Services, Inc., 1991).

Twelve Steps and Twelve Traditions of Overeaters Anonymous (Torrance, Calif.: Overeaters Anonymous, Inc., 1993).

Stop Letting Food Control You.

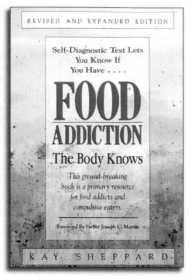

Here food addiction is defined, trigger foods are identified and consequences of food addiction are revealed. A lifetime eating plan is presented, which demonstrates how to stick with a healthful food plan for the long term.

Code 276X • paperback • $9.95

Kay Sheppard has helped countless people free themselves from the roller coaster ride of food addiction—let her help you or anyone you know who has a problem with food.

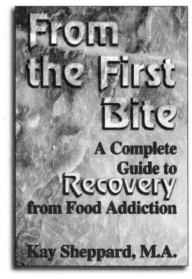

Code 7540 • paperback • $11.95